L.V. Rutgers

# Subterranean Rome

## In Search of the Roots of Christianity
## in the Catacombs of the Eternal City

PEETERS

*Photo credits*

Fig. 1, 4, 12, 13,14, 16, 17, 18, 21, 27, 29, 30, 45, 48, 50 author; 2, 5, 11, 32 Wilpert; 3, 9, 19 Marucchi; 6 JTS; 8, 20, 23, 24, 26, 31, 34, 35, 37, 39, 41, 42, 43, 44, 47 PCAS; 10, 15, 49 de Rossi; 22, 25, 40, 46 Reekmans; 28, 33, 38 DAI Rome.

D.2000/0602/62
ISBN 90-429-0857-2 (Peeters Leuven)
©2000-Uitgeverij Peeters, Bondgenotenlaan 153, B-3000 Leuven

# Subterranean Rome

*In Search of the Roots of Christianity in the Catacombs of the Eternal City*

# Introduction

The catacombs – the long subterranean galleries into which the early Christian community of Rome buried its dead – have always fascinated visitors to Rome. Containing the tombs of some of early Christianity's most famous representatives, along with the graves of tens of thousands of less famous believers, the catacombs of Rome are awe-inspiring places that cannot fail to impress anyone who dares to enter them. Visiting the catacombs around the middle of the fourth century A.D., the church father Jerome described his impressions of the catacombs in a manner even modern visitors will find appropriate: "while it is pitch dark, the words of the prophet seem to come true: 'may they go down alive into Sheol" (Psalm 55:15); only occasionally light enters from above that helps to diminish the horrors of darkness; and when one returns step by step and the darkness of night surrounds you entirely, the following verse of Virgil comes to mind: "Everywhere dread fills my heart; the very silence too dismays" (Aeneid II, 755).

Given the importance of these monuments for the history of Christianity, and taking into account the impressive array of archaeological materials that have been preserved in them, it is not really surprising that the catacombs of Rome have always exerted such a strong fascination on virtually everyone who knows about their existence. There simply exists no other place where such a high concentration of early Christian tombs, funerary inscriptions, and wall paintings can be found. Nor is there any other place where such remains have been preserved in such quantities and so well. If one wants to immerse oneself in the world of early Christianity, to engage in the study of its physical remains, or to explore its theology, a visit to the catacombs will prove to be the most effective and rewarding way of accomplishing this. One needs to do no more than to descend several flights of stairs to travel back in time and enter a fascinating world – a world that, in many respects, has long ceased to exist.

Since their rediscovery in the late sixteenth century, much archaeological research has been carried out in the catacombs of Rome. As a result of all this research, it has become possible to answer a whole series of questions that have long baffled all those interested in the catacombs and their history. We now know, for example, how the catacombs originated, what kind of people were buried in them, and what beliefs inspired those who ordered the wall paintings and other works of art that survive in these catacombs in such astonishing numbers. Such research has also helped us to debunk several myths about the catacombs, including the idea that the catacombs were constructed underground specifically to help Rome's early Christian community hide from those who persecuted them.

Considering all the progress that has been made in this area – especially during the last thirty years – it is disturbing to note that few of these new insights that have been gained have entered into the more popular literature on the topic, let alone the guidebooks. Readers of such literature have to content themselves with theories no serious scholar would even dream to uphold. Unless one wants to immerse oneself in specialized excavations reports, it is virtually impossible to find publications that provide the non-specialist with up-to-date, digestible information. The lack of a reliable, yet readable introduction in English to the archaeology and art from the early catacombs of Rome is all the more peculiar when one realizes that the year 2000 is a Holy Year. During this year, a series of ecclesiastical celebrations will take place in which the catacombs will play an important part.

The purpose of this book is to fill the just-mentioned vacuum. Its aim is to provide readers with up-to-date and easy-to-access information on the catacombs of Rome. As such, it can be read either in preparation for a visit to the catacombs of Rome, or as a guide book while in Rome. It can also be used as a work of reference, not only by tourists and pilgrims, but also by all those who would like to familiarize themselves with the present state of affairs in catacomb archaeology (such as students of art history, early Christian archaeology, and church history). A selected bibliography at the end of the book provides guidance to those who wish to pursue further reading or research on the catacombs.

To date, some sixty catacombs have been discovered in and around Rome. Only a few of these (mostly the larger ones) are accessible to the general public. Inasmuch as it would make little sense to discuss extensively archaeological remains the majority of tourists and pilgrims to Rome will not be in a position to see, the author of this book has tried to illustrate the most important concepts of catacomb archaeology by referring to those remains that can be viewed by all.

To present the available evidence as concisely and coherently as possible, the book has been divided into four chapters.

Chapter I discusses the history of research. Familiarity with this history is important because it helps the reader to understand why catacomb archaeology has developed in the way it did and why certain questions have traditionally been considered more important than others.

Chapter II focuses on the archaeology of the catacombs. In this chapter, we will not only discuss how the catacombs emerged and what archaeological evidence can be brought to bear on this issue. We will also consider some of the methodological problems that make catacomb archaeology such a complex and challenging form of archaeology.

Chapter III deals with the genesis of early Christian art as it can be reconstructed on the basis of the remains preserved in the catacombs of Rome.

Chapter IV is a guide that contains a short description of all the catacombs that are freely accessible. It also contains practical information concerning the location, opening hours and so on of the catacombs in question.

The appendix contains information concerning the Jewish catacombs of Rome as well as the inscriptions that have been found in both the Jewish and Christian catacombs of Rome. A selected bibliography and a glossary conclude the book.

# CHAPTER 1

# The Discovery of the Catacombs

## Introduction

Much of what we know about the early Christian catacombs of Rome is the result of painstaking archaeological research that has been carried out in them over a period of more than four hundred years. As a result of this research, we now know of the existence of some sixty early Christian catacombs or subterranean burial places in and around Rome. Some of these catacombs are quite small. Others, however, are impressive monuments that consist of many miles of underground galleries. Some of these larger catacombs take on such huge dimensions that they are true underground necropoleis, "cities of the dead," in which one can wonder for hours on end (fig. 1).

Given the enormous size of these underground burial places and considering the importance of the archaeological materials they contain, it is hard to imagine that until their rediscovery in the late sixteenth century, people knew very little about the catacombs.

Yet, there was a time when no one seems to have cared much for the early Christian catacombs of Rome. For more than six centuries, from the ninth through the sixteenth century, the once famous early Christian catacombs of Rome had all but fallen into oblivion. Upon closer consideration, however, it is perhaps not all that strange that for long periods of time the catacombs were hidden almost entirely from public view. After having been used for burial uninterruptedly from the early second through the late fifth century

Fig. 1. Gallery in the catacombs with wall graves (*loculi*).

A.D., the early medieval inhabitants of Rome stopped burying in them because they preferred other burial customs. During this time, Rome saw the emergence of the practice of burying one's dead in or near churches. Unlike the burial slots that were hidden away in the deep underground galleries of the catacombs, graves of this new type were always located on the surface and within city limits.

Still another factor that contributed to the lack of interest in the catacombs has to do with what might be called an early form of tourism. From the fifth through the ninth century, it was customary for pilgrims from all over Europe to come to Rome and visit the catacombs. There they wanted to pay homage to the graves of early Christian martyrs, that is of those champions of the Christian faith who had given up their lives voluntarily and who had frequently died violent deaths, all for the greater glory of the Church. In the course of the eighth century, however, church authorities began to remove the mortal remains of these martyrs from the catacombs, and to rebury them in churches located at various points within the city of Rome. Although such *translationes* or transfers of martyrial remains made life easier for those wishing to pray in the presence of these remains, it also resulted, at the same time, in an ever-stronger decrease in the number of people who visited the catacombs. By the late ninth century the catacombs were no longer an integral part of the monuments every pilgrim to Rome would visit, and even the local population began to forget about their existence. Thus, after a period of seven centuries during which they had been used and visited intensively, there followed a period of seven centuries during which all was quiet in the early Christian catacombs of Rome.

With the rediscovery of the early Christian catacombs of Rome in the late sixteenth century begins a new period in the history of these magnificent monuments of early Christianity – a period characterized by a renewed interest and by intensive research. While during this time systematic explorations of the countryside around Rome led to the discovery of one catacomb after another, research within the catacombs themselves resulted in the discovery of archaeological materials that turned out to illustrate the history of early Christianity in ways never before imagined. Yet it was not the impressiveness of these monuments themselves nor the beauty of the artistic materials they contained that mesmerized people. Rather, it was the intellectual climate at the time that contributed to turning the rediscovery of the early Christian catacombs of Rome into an event that had profound ramifications on the way people viewed the history of Christianity in general and the position of the Church of Rome in particular.

To understand how it could happen that the rediscovery of the catacombs had the effect of a tidal wave, affecting the minds of scholars, theologians, and the general public alike, it is necessary to consider briefly the events that helped to shape the intellectual and religious climate in sixteenth century Europe. It may be recalled that earlier in that century, the Continent had seen the emergence of Protestantism. This led to much unrest. The Catholic-Protestant controversy manifested itself in various ways. Protestant theologians soon adopted the habit of expressing their disagreement by writing historical studies. In such studies they tried to show that the Church of Rome had long condoned and accepted liturgical practices and beliefs that were entirely unknown to the first Christian communities and that had come into existence only at a later stage in the history of Christianity. Protestant thinkers viewed such practices and beliefs as deviations. Their extensive philological research into the most ancient writings of the early Church served, therefore, to document the extent to which these deviations had changed the true nature of Christianity. In their view, Catholic doctrine had corrupted Western Christendom to the bone.

Even though it took some time for Catholic scholars to assimilate the results of these Protestant philological studies, they were quick in realizing that such studies could easily harm the Church of Rome. A Catholic answer finally appeared in the years 1588-1607. It took the form of an impressive *Ecclesiastical History from the Birth of Christ till the Year 1198*. Consisting of twelve fat volumes, this history was written in Latin by Cesare Baronio (1538-1607), a priest and one of the better-known intellectuals of the period.

Taking into account the purpose for which Baronio's *Ecclesiastical History* had been written, it is not surprising to note that this work belongs to the same apologetic genre as those to which it responds. Yet, Baronio's monumental work differed in one important respect from all the other apologetic literature that had preceded it: in it could be found a new sense of self-confidence. This sense of self-confidence was not merely the byproduct or even a function of the Catholic Church's vigorous response to Protestantism known as the Counter-reformation. It resulted from the conviction that one could actually prove beyond reasonable doubt that the Catholic view of the history of Christianity as propounded in works such as Baronio's *Ecclesiastical History* was the only correct one.

It is not hard to identify which event stood at the basis of this conviction: it was the rediscovery of the early Christian catacombs of Rome. In 1578 workers in the Vigna (vineyard) Sanchez, to the North of Rome, accidentally came across a cavity that, upon closer investigation, turned out to be a catacomb in which one of the earliest Christian communities in ancient Rome had laid to rest its dead. This discovery was quite unexpected and was to have a profound impact on these apologetic discussions. All of a sudden, scholars found themselves face to face with the actual physical remains left behind by the early Christian community of ancient Rome. Thus, instead of being confronted with the writings of the early Church that were often hard to interpret, scholars now found themselves in a unique position to directly access and touch the physical remains left behind by the first Christians. Such finds, they believed, spoke for themselves and were, therefore, easy to interpret. Here, to their great delight, they had at their disposal the world of the common folk, the Christians of rank-and-file, the "real thing."

It hardly needs stressing that discoveries such as the one in the Vigna Sanchez provided Catholic intellectuals with new and rather deadly ammunition. Pointing to the wall paintings that had been preserved in the catacombs, Catholic scholars argued that art and artistic renderings of Christian beliefs and concepts had always been an integral part of Christianity. Thus such scholars were armed with good evidence to argue that the iconoclasm of the Protestants that had led to the destruction of many a Catholic church in Northern Europe, was not in the least consistent with the ideas and ideals prevalent among the earliest Christian communities. Along similar lines, on the basis of representations encountered in the catacombs, Catholic scholars had reason to argue that the veneration of the Virgin Mary was not a recent Catholic invention, but rather that it was an original Christian practice that went back to the earliest beginnings of the Christian faith (fig. 2). How Catholic scholars of the time perceived the catacombs can best be summed up by citing one of them who remarked that the catacombs really were "arsenals from which to take the weapons to combat heretics, and in particular the iconoclasts, impugners of sacred images, of which the cemeteries are plenty."

Fig. 2. Drawing from the time of the Counterreformation. Even though the figures represented here (Madonna with child and scene with martyrs) render paintings discovered in the catacombs, details that do not appear in the original (such as the halos) were added, thus illustrating how the ideals of the Counterreformation influenced society at large.

Taking into account these developments, one can begin to understand why the rediscovery of the early Christian catacombs of Rome made such an impression on people all over Europe. The early Christian catacombs of Rome were not just seen as the rudimentary remains of a Christian community that had long ceased to exist. Rather, they were viewed as monuments that could provide scholars with useful evidence in debates that at heart had little to do with early Christian history and everything with sixteenth century theology. Because the evidence from the catacombs was not normally allowed to stand on its own, but was considered only in terms of its potential usefulness in theological controversies, it was customary, from the earliest beginnings of catacomb archaeology, to look at the archaeological evidence from the catacombs from a very specific angle, and from this angle only. In the sixteenth century and beyond, studying the art from the catacombs and the mortal remains of Rome's earliest Christian communities was not just a form of antiquarianism. It was an honorable theological occupation, one that quickly earned itself the designation "sacred archaeology."

The fact that catacomb archaeology originated in counter-reformist Europe has had an enormous impact on the way this particular area of scholarly investigation developed subsequently. The apologetic atmosphere characteristic of Rome in the time of the Counterreformation determined the kind of evidence scholars were willing to consider, the kind of questions they were willing to ask, and the kind of methodologies they were willing to apply. The specific emphases in the writings of the first generation of archaeologists working in the catacombs of Rome determined, in turn, the work of later generations of archaeologists. Even though slight shifts in emphasis can be determined in the work of such later generations, it is remarkable to see how insignificant such shifts really were within the larger scheme of things. Thus, even in studies written in the late nineteenth and early twentieth century, it is possible to discern traces of apologetic arguments that were first formulated during the time of the Counter-reformation. That this is so will become evident in the pages that follow. In them we will analyze the writings of scholars whose work has been of great importance for the study of catacomb archaeology. To review these writings briefly is particularly worthwhile because it will allow us to see why catacomb archaeology has developed the way it has, and why certain types of questions have traditionally been considered more important than others.

## Antonio Bosio (1575-1629)

The discovery of an early Christian catacomb in the Vigna Sanchez in 1578 marks the beginning of a period characterized by a renewed interest in the catacombs of ancient Rome. In the years following the Vigna Sanchez discovery, scholars now began to search specifically for the physical remains left behind by Rome's early Christian community. Consequently, many other early Christian catacombs were discovered during these early years of catacomb archaeology. Yet, even though research was henceforth carried out on a larger scale than ever before, much of this research was not systematic. Thus, although the catacombs were rescued from oblivion in the late sixteenth century, this did not automatically mean that information that now became available was reliable. To ensure that the catacombs would not once again be forgotten after the initial excitement about their rediscovery had worn off, systematic research was necessary. One man, known by posterity as "Columbus of the catacombs," would carry out such research. His name was Antonio Bosio (1575-1629).

Bosio was born on the island of Malta. As a young man, he came to Rome to study law. After finishing his studies, he began to practice law, only to discover that this was not his true calling. In 1593 some friends of his took him on a tour that would change his life completely. This trip took Bosio to the Domitilla catacomb – one of the largest early Christian catacombs of Rome, and one that can still be visited today (fig. 3).

As is evident from a report Bosio composed later, the visit to the Domitilla catacomb made a deep and lasting impression on the young man. The vastness of the underground galleries in this catacomb was such that it "seemed that these grottoes were never-ending...from central grottoes there departed galleries in all directions of the wind, galleries that, in turn, seemed to divide themselves into thousands of new galleries." Wishing to retrieve "a complete early Christian inscription," Bosio and his friends proceeded deep into the subsoil of the Roman countryside. There they discovered, to their great distress, that their candles had burnt up and that they had failed to bring enough candles to help them find their way back to the entrance to this enormous underground cemetery. Considering that even today it is virtually impossible to find the entrance of a catacomb without some form of lighting, Bosio was not too far off in fearing that he and his friends might very well end up "polluting this holy monument with our impure bodies." Only at this point it occurred to Bosio that "this was, after all, the first time that we entered these enormous, unexplored cemeteries, and that we, inexperienced as we were, had come without the equipment necessary for such a peregrination." Long after the sun had set, Bosio and his friends finally managed to find the opening by which they had originally entered the catacomb. Not surprisingly, this whole affair impressed Bosio greatly. Never again he

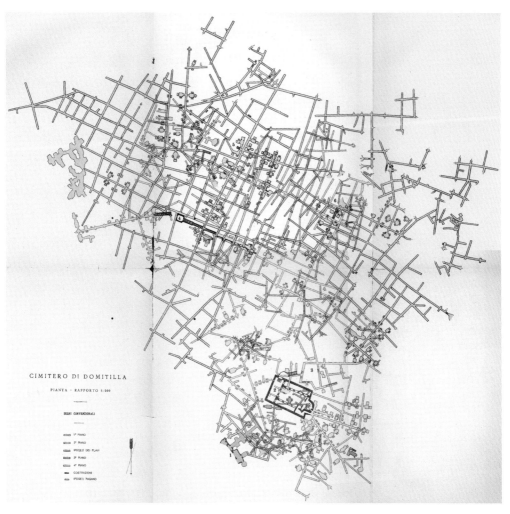

Fig. 3. Plan of the Domitilla catacomb. The various levels in the catacomb have been marked with color.

would dream of entering a catacomb without the necessary supplies such as "large quantities of candles," ropes, shovels and the like.

Bosio's visit to the Domitilla catacomb marks the beginning of a new period in his life. From now on, Bosio would dedicate himself entirely to the study of the early Christian catacombs of Rome. In one respect in particular, Bosio's work differs from that of those who preceded him: Bosio was thoroughly systematic. This preference for a systematic approach explains, among other things, why he studied the catacombs in the way he did. Realizing that the early Christian catacombs of Rome were (and are) mostly located along the highways that connected Rome with its Empire, Bosio decided that the best way to inventory the available evidence was to make a division into highway-zones. Thus, in 1593, in the same year he first visited the Domitilla catacomb, Bosio began to investigate all those early Christian cemeteries located along the Via Tiburtina (the road to Tivoli). In the following year, he continued his investigations with a study of all the early Christian catacombs along the Via Appia, the Via Labicana, the Via Nomentina, the two Vias Salaria, and the Via Flaminia (fig. 4). In 1595 he turned his attention to the Via Ostiense, in 1596 to the Via Latina, and in 1600 to the Via Portuense. Having thus completed his project of systematic survey, Bosio would occasionally return to the catacombs, and he would also investigate catacombs that had been accidentally discovered in the meantime. One such catacomb was the Jewish catacomb in the city quarter of Monteverde, south of Trastevere (now destroyed).

As Bosio was mapping the Roman countryside and studying the catacombs, including the archaeological materials they contained, he also began to inventory ancient literary sources bearing on Rome's early Christian community, the cult of the

Fig. 4. Via Appia Antica, the oldest consular road near Rome. Alongside this road, the remains of pagan mausolea can be found. Below these, early Christian catacombs such as the Sebastiano and Callisto catacombs were constructed.

martyrs, and late antique burial practices. That the available literary evidence on these topics was enormous follows from the fact that the notes Bosio took during his study of these sources make up no less that four very substantial volumes (fig. 5).

Of all the literary sources Bosio was able to put his hands on during the long hours he spent in libraries and archives, there was one type of literature that soon began to attract his special attention: the itineraries. These itineraries were travel guides that had come into existence in the early Middle Ages. Composed in Latin, they had been written by and for pilgrims and served to give these pilgrims an idea of the sights they could expect to encounter in and around Rome. They also contained concisely formulated information on how to find such sights. Although such itineraries are not very interesting from a literary point of view, they are very useful from a scholarly point of view in that they often contain information that cannot be found in any other literary source. To give but one example of the type of information they contain, and

Fig. 5. Page from Antonio Bosio's sketchbook. These sketches which are based on wall paintings found by Bosio in the Priscilla catacomb, include a representation of a Madonna with child, a good shepherd, and of people praying.

of the way in which this information has been phrased, the following passage may be cited. It derives from a seventh-century pilgrim travel guide entitled *Concerning the Places of the Holy Martyrs that are located Outside the City of Rome*: "Along the Via Labicana there lies the Church of the Holy Helena in which her dead body can also be found; there also the following saints lay sound asleep: Peter, Marcellinus, Tiburtius, the thirty holy soldiers, Gorgonius, Genuinus, Maximus, the four Coronati (crowned ones), namely Claudius, Nicostratus, Simpronianus, Castorius, Simplicius; there and in the crypts under the surface there also lay buried an innumerable number of martyrs."[1]

---

[1]    Helena was the mother of the Emperor Constantine, the first Christian emperor (although modern scholarly opinion is divided on how genuinely Christian Constantine really was). Along the Via Labicana (today Via Casilina), Constantine erected a mausoleum for his mother. The catacomb located near this mausoleum is known by the name of *ad duas lauros* ("near the two laurels") or the catacombs of Marcellinus and Peter.

Although passages such as these may strike the modern readers as rather boring, it hardly needs stressing that they contained information that was, from Bosio's point of view, extremely important and interesting: the itineraries provided Bosio with a unique opportunity to help find early Christian catacombs the location of which had been forgotten long ago. In addition, the itineraries also contained useful information to determine which martyrs or saints had been buried in which catacomb. Thus, the itineraries not merely provided Bosio something to go by; they also provided him an essential framework that permitted him, at the end of his career, to draw a coherent picture of how the early Christian catacombs of Rome had originated, how they had been used, and how, in the Middle Ages, they had once again fallen into disuse.

Considering the importance attached to the catacombs by the Roman Church authorities in general, and by the Church's apologists in particular, it was only natural for the Roman Catholic Church to take a lively interest in Bosio's work. Cesare Baronio, the famous Catholic historian mentioned previously, for example, loved to accompany Bosio during his subterranean wanderings. In light of what has been said about the way the catacombs were viewed in the time of the Counterreformation, it should not surprise us to observe that Baronio found such visits highly rewarding, or, to cite Bosio who commented on a joint trip to the Marcellinus and Peter-catacomb, "truly satisfying." In the catacombs, Bosio could show Baronio the hard evidence the latter had been looking for so desperately and for so many years: monumental inscriptions, erected in the 360s A.D. by Pope Damasus, that marked the graves of Christianity's most famous martyrs and that commemorated their deeds in the form of long inscriptions in verse. Baronio was ever so thankful. Now he felt he could prove definitively that there existed a direct link between the Christian communities of old and the Roman Catholic Church of his own day. It inspired him to compose not just historical studies, but also other works, such as the important *Martyrologium Romanum*, a liturgical book in calendar form containing short descriptions of the lives of the martyrs, the first copy of which was presented in 1598 by Baronio himself to Pope Sixtus V.

Like Baronio, Bosio too was a writer who wanted to see in print the results of his many years of painstaking research in the early Christian catacombs of Rome. The publication of Bosio's monumental *Roma Sotterranea* (*Subterranean Rome*), which did not appear until two years after his death in 1632, was, obviously, an important event (fig. 6). This book, written by the one whose knowledge of the catacombs was unsurpassed, instantly became a standard work of reference; it would remain so for more than two hundred years, well into the nineteenth century. A translation of Bosio's Italian study into Latin which first appeared in 1651 seems to have enjoyed particular popularity, as is evident from the various reprints that succeeded one another in rapid succession and from the preparation of a pocket edition that first came on the market in 1671.

Bosio's *Subterranean Rome* is a truly monumental study, one in which even modern-day scholars can find much useful information. It consists of four parts and includes a full description of early Christian burial customs and the cult of the martyrs (Part I), a systematic description of all early catacombs known in Bosio's time (Parts II and III), and a discussion of the art that can be found in the catacombs (Part IV). What makes Bosio's tome especially interesting is the many illustrations that can be found in the 656 pages of text Bosio produced. Such illustrations permitted scholars, and especially those who were unable to visit the catacombs, to get an idea of what the art from the catacombs looked like, and of how the subterranean galleries of these underground cemeteries had been arranged. What makes the illustrations in Bosio's *Subterranean Rome* interesting from our modern point of view

Fig. 6. Title page of Antonio Bosio's *Roma sotterranea*. The engraving included in this title page helps to stress the idea that the catacombs served as places of refuge.

is that in some cases they are the only information we have on wall paintings that have disappeared in the centuries following Bosio's investigations. One may fairly conclude, therefore, that with the publication of his *Subterranean Rome* Bosio rendered a great service, not only to his contemporaries, but also to posterity.

Considering the seriousness with which Bosio engaged in the study of catacomb archaeology – a type of archaeological research of which he may rightly be called the founding father – one might be tempted to forget that Bosio too could not always avoid being influenced by the ideas that had led to so much commotion in Roman Catholic circles. Like some of his more outspoken Catholic contemporaries, Bosio also believed that in the catacombs there was to be found evidence that could be used to document that the Roman Catholic Church of his day was the exclusive heir to and a direct successor of one of the oldest early Christian communities of the world. Moreover, by exploring the cult of the martyrs in the systematic fashion he did, Bosio laid the foundation for what was to become one of the most widespread myths of catacomb archaeology, namely the idea that the early Christian catacombs of Rome had served as place of refuge for the early Christian community of Rome during the anti-Christian persecutions of the first three centuries. In spite of the no-nonsense approach that generally characterizes Bosio's scholarly work, one cannot but conclude, therefore, that in the end Bosio too was a child of his age.

Taking into account the Counterreformist ideas that lurk below the surface in Bosio's book, it is not at all surprising that Protestant scholars soon began to criticize Bosio and then began to reject the latter's views on how the art from the catacombs might be interpreted. A brief review of the arguments of these critics is in place here. As we will now see, such critics began to raise issues that are quite pertinent and that continue to intrigue even modern day scholars who specialize in catacomb archaeology.

## Jacques Basnage (1653-1723)

One of Bosio's fiercest critics was a French Huguenot who had left France and had settled in the Netherlands. There he published, in French, a substantial *History of the Jews from Jesus Christ to the Present* (1706). This publication – the first comprehensive history of the Jewish people since Antiquity – is a peculiar work, that is, as long as one is not aware of the apologetic tendencies underlying it. Containing a long and detailed description of the sufferings of the Jewish people through the ages, its purpose was to blame the Catholic Church as being solely responsible for these sufferings. It is important to note, however, that Basnage was not interested in Jewish history per se. Quite the contrary. Basnage cared little for the Jews and did not really like the Jewish religion. Rather, he saw the sufferings of the Jews as a metaphor for the sufferings that he and his co-religionists, the Huguenots, had endured at the hands of the Catholic Church. Thus, in reality, Basnage's *History of the Jews* was nothing but a long and detailed attack on the Church of Rome that had consciously been packaged in such a way as to draw attention away from the people most interested in this attack, namely the Huguenot community (fig. 7).

Although the archaeological evidence that had been discovered in the early Christian catacombs of Rome interested Basnage only to the extent that a discussion of this evidence could serve to criticize his Catholic contemporaries, it is nonetheless worthwhile to review the arguments Basnage put forward. Interestingly enough, in his analysis of the archaeological materials from the early Christian catacombs of Rome

Fig. 7. Engraving of Giovanni del Pian, illustrating a Jewish funerary cortege dating to the period in which Basnage wrote his *History of the Jewish People*.

and, more specifically, of the ways in which these materials could be interpreted, Basnage reached conclusions no subsequent scholar could afford to neglect, as we will now see.

It has already been observed that through the publication of Bosio's *Subterranean Rome* scholars were able to familiarize themselves in a comprehensive fashion with the archaeological materials from the early Christian catacombs of Rome, with the relevant ancient literary sources, as well as with several theories regarding how the early Christian catacombs of Rome had come into existence and how they had developed. In the course of his *History of the Jews*, Basnage proceeded to inspect several of these theories, only to conclude that the most important ones had to be rejected on the basis of logical reasoning. Thus Basnage questioned the idea that catacombs were a typically Christian invention. He argued that at least until the fourth century A.D. the Christian community had simply been too small to justify the construction of large underground cemeteries such as the catacombs. Instead, Basnage believed that others had taken the first step in constructing the catacombs of Rome, and he pointed to pagan archaeological evidence that had been discovered in and around the catacombs in an attempt to identify the people who were really responsible for inventing this type of funerary construction. For that reason, Basnage believed that the Christians had merely adapted an already existing way of burying the dead. Using dated inscriptions, Basnage further argued that Christians had utilized the catacombs for burial in a systematic fashion only from the fourth century A.D. onwards, and not already in the first century A.D., as his Catholic counterparts maintained. Basnage also rejected the idea that the catacombs served as places of refuge for a persecuted Christian community. Taking into account their location, namely along Rome's major highways, Basnage found it highly unlikely to suppose that the existence of these enormous underground cemeteries could have remained a secret for long.

Having thus questioned some of the theories that had attained great respectability in Catholic circles, Basnage then proceeded to criticize the Church's interpretation of the martyrial remains it believed had been preserved in the catacombs. Basnage was willing to admit to the possibility that martyrs had been laid to rest in the catacombs, that is, once in a while. Yet, Basnage was not so sure as to how to recognize the burial spot of such martyrs or how to identify them in ways that went beyond pure speculation. "Provided that one is at all able to identify the remains of martyrs as such, how then can one determine that one is in fact dealing with the remains of orthodox martyrs rather than heterodox ones, such as Donatists or Arians?" Basnage wondered.[2]

Looking somewhat more closely at Basnage's arguments, it is interesting to see that in a number of cases, he seems to have reached conclusions similar to those reached by modern scholarship. Recent research has shown, for example, that the early Christian catacombs of Rome did not come into existence until the late second or early third century A.D. Along similar lines, subsequent study has revealed that the catacombs never served as places of refuge. Recent research has also helped to underscore Basnage's point that not every bit of archaeological evidence should automatically be taken to point to the presence of early Christian martyrs. Thus, earlier this century, chemical analysis has helped to establish that the red substance contained in ampoules found in the catacombs should not be regarded as traces of blood and thus as evidence indicating the presence of a martyr's grave. The red color in these ampoules is nothing but traces of red pigment. Its presence tells us nothing about the early Christian cult of the martyrs.

Now, of course, it must be admitted that Basnage could not be certain that in a number of cases he was right. After all, Basnage did not reach his conclusions on the basis of studying the catacombs in person, but rather by means of sound reasoning. He merely utilized, in a rather ingenious

---

[2]    Donatism and Arianism were heterodox movements within early Christianity. Both movements got into conflict with the Church of Rome, the Donatists because they questioned the legitimacy of the Roman Church as a result of the latter's concessive attitude during the great anti-Christian persecutions in North Africa in the early fourth century A.D., and the Arians because they did not agree that Jesus was "of the same substance" as God.

manner, the evidence Bosio had put at his disposal by publishing his *Subterranean Rome*!

Basnage's critical-literary approach explains why many of his theories did not, in the end, convince his Roman contemporaries. They regarded Basnage as an outsider, as someone who had no working experience in the catacombs of Rome, and therefore as someone one did not need to take seriously. Consequently, Basnage's remarks did not trigger new research in the catacombs themselves. In Rome, and in Catholic circles in general, Bosio's theories still ruled supreme. It would take more than a century before scholars began to resume archaeological fieldwork in the early Christian catacombs of Rome. What was needed for this was a second Bosio. Such a person finally appeared on the scene almost a century after Basnage had passed away. His name was Gionanni Battista de Rossi.

### Giovanni Battista de Rossi (1822-1894)

Just as Bosio can be considered the founding father of catacomb archaeology, de Rossi can be regarded as the founder of the modern-scholarly approach to catacomb archaeology. To cite the words of a contemporary of de Rossi: "Before de Rossi early Christian archaeology was nothing but a pasttime for amateurs, since de Rossi it has become a field for serious scholarly investigation."

Looking at the biography of both men, it is interesting to see how much Bosio and de Rossi had in common. Just like Bosio before him, de Rossi studied law. Just like Bosio, de Rossi did not want to pursue a career as a lawyer after having completed his studies, but instead decided to devote his full attention to the study of the early Christian antiquities of Rome. Ever since he had received, at age eleven, a copy of Bosio's *Subterranean Rome* as a birthday present, de Rossi had dreamt of stepping into Bosio's footsteps.

Given all that Bosio had accomplished in the study of the catacombs by his combined archaeological and philological approach, it was only natural for de Rossi to take Bosio's methodology as a starting point, in an attempt to perfect it and reach conclusions that would stand the test of time. Like Bosio, he recognized the importance of archaeological fieldwork and spent a considerable amount of his time underground, exposing and excavating burial chambers and complex networks of underground galleries. With Bosio, de Rossi also shared an interest for the itineraries, or medieval travel accounts we already discussed briefly. In order to document the available source materials as completely as possible, de Rossi made a point of travelling to libraries all over Europe to study the itineraries in manuscript form. Thus he laid the basis for the first reliable scholarly edition of these itineraries.

The search for the graves of the martyrs also plays a significant role in the work of de Rossi, but the emphasis he placed on this evidence is different from that which one encounters in the work of Bosio. We have seen that what mattered most to Bosio in his study of martyrial remains was to craft a link between the early Church and the Church of his own day. Such apologetic concerns are almost entirely absent in the work of de Rossi. De Rossi's interest in the graves of the martyrs was sparked by his conviction that he could unravel the history of the catacombs by focusing on this evidence specifically. De Rossi's line of reasoning was as follows: if, de Rossi argued, one can identify the grave of a martyr in a catacomb, and if one then succeeds in identifying the name of this martyr in ancient literary sources, then one should be in a position to establish a sound chronology for that part of the catacomb in which the martyr in question has been buried. De Rossi believed that the grave of such martyrs could best be found by focusing on those galleries in the catacombs where much building activity had taken place. That was a logical supposition. After all, such building activity naturally resulted from the wish to embellish the graves of famous martyrs as well as the need to accommodate as many visitors as possible (all those pilgrims who came to pay their respect to the tombs of the holy martyrs, itinerary in hand).

It was de Rossi himself who proved the usefulness of the above hypothesis, for example in his work in the Calixtus catacomb, one of the largest early Christian catacombs in Rome. Working there for many years, de Rossi succeeded in unravelling the chronology of this catacomb by concentrating on the excavation of a series of crypts and burial chambers where much building activity had taken place and in which, as de Rossi was able to prove on the basis of inscriptions, a number of historical figures had been laid to rest. De Rossi's most important discovery in the Calixtus catacomb occurred in 1854, with the unearthing of the so-called "crypt of the popes." This crypt, which can still be visited today, contained an inscription that had been placed there in the course of the fourth century by Pope Damasus and that de Rossi found fractured in no less than 125 pieces (fig. 8). In it was commemorated a whole series of third-century popes, that is, of ecclesiastical dignitaries that were also known from ancient literary sources. It hardly needs stressing that the discovery of the "crypt of the popes" and the long inscription it contained was an exciting discovery indeed. It enabled de Rossi to place the construction history of the Calixtus catacomb within a much larger historical framework than had been possible ever before.

As a result of his discoveries, and thanks to his methodologies as expounded in his three-volume tour de force *La Roma sotterranea cristiana* (*Subterranean Christian Rome*), published in the years 1864-1877, de Rossi succeeded in getting both scholars and the general public interested in the early Christian catacombs of Rome. That in itself was a major accomplishment, and one of de Rossi's great contributions to catacomb archaeology. Even though scholars had always continued to write about the catacombs after Bosio died in 1632,

Fig. 8. Crypt of the popes. In the background can be seen part of the famous inscription that was installed there by Pope Damasus and that was later rediscovered and reconstructed by de Rossi.

the study of the catacombs had nonetheless become a some-what parochial affair as time went by. Even in Catholic circles, catacomb archaeology had lost much of its appeal as soon as the spirit of the Counterreformation began to yield, in due course, to the writings of less polemical thinkers and theologians. If we are to believe a report in the *Giornale di Roma* of 1854, Pope Pius IX, upon visiting the just discovered "crypt of the popes," is credited with having asked de Rossi: "Is it really true what you are telling me; is it not possible that we are dealing with some sort of an illusion here?" To which de Rossi is said to have responded that his discoveries were not about illusions, but about hard data, such as inscriptions. If, de Rossi continued, the Pope would only take the effort and help him in putting together the fragmented inscription, then the names of those that had preceded him, Pope Pius IX, would readily appear (fig. 9). Thus it happened. When the names of all those illustrious men who had succeeded the *princeps apostolorum* began to appear, the Pope burst into tears.[3]

Fig. 9. Relief commemorating the visit of Pope Pius IX to the Domitilla catacomb. De Rossi who comments on his discoveries, stands to the Pope's right.

---

[3]   The *princeps apostolorum* (literally "the first of the apostles") is a reference to Peter who, according to Catholic tradition, was the first pope and founder of the Papacy.

De Rossi's work in the catacombs resulted in a number of important discoveries. Not only did he discover catacombs that had been unknown previously, thus bringing the total of known catacombs to around 60 (Bosio had known of the existence of 30 catacombs only). De Rossi also helped to dispel other myths about the catacombs that had sprung up in the course of time. Whereas other scholars had argued that the catacombs first came into existence at a time when the apostles Paul and Peter had been active in Rome (the middle of the first century A.D.), de Rossi collected incontrovertible evidence to show that not a single catacomb had been dug before the reign of the Flavian emperors or even the emperor Trajan (late first and early second century A.D.). Further research has shown, incidentally, that even this dating is too early.

Throughout his career, de Rossi had been conscious about not getting involved in the apologetic and theological discussions that had characterized the field of catacomb archaeology since its inception in the time of the Counterreformation. "I am an archaeologist, not a theologian," he once stated emphatically. "I only tell you what I know, about the rest I do not care," he had said on another occasion. And when people reproached him for secretly conspiring with the Protestants, de Rossi commented that such people tried to discredit his orthodoxy by means of gossip and insinuations for a very simply reason only: the poor chaps had not been able to find fault with his scholarly publications.

Although such evidence seems to suggest, at first sight, that the apologetic arguments of old did not play a role in the work of de Rossi, such a conclusion is not entirely correct. If one reads between the lines, one soon discovers that de Rossi too could not free himself entirely from the views that had circulated in Catholic circles for at least three centuries.

Thus, de Rossi believed that the early Christian catacombs of Rome were truly "Roman Catholic burial places," in which people had been laid to rest whose religious beliefs could best be described as pure and untainted (fig. 10). Along similar lines, in the introduction to the *Bulletin of Christian Archaeology* – a journal that de Rossi founded – de Rossi made explicit how he viewed the study of the catacombs, namely as "antidote against all sorts of errors and as such given to us by divine providence." Statements such as these help to explain how it was possible for de Rossi to view the study of the catacombs and of early Christian antiquities as a type of endeavor that held one promise in particular: to bring about "new victories for the truth and for the (Catholic) faith."

We have had occasion already to comment on how much de Rossi had in common with Bosio. It light of what has been said about their discoveries, it is hardly surprising to note that the similarity between both scholars also extends to the influence they were able to exert on subsequent generations of scholars. Both scholars succeeded in placing the early Christian catacombs on the intellectual map in a thoroughly scholarly fashion. Through their methodologies, Bosio and

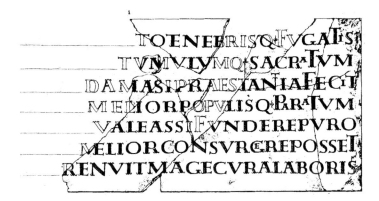

Fig. 10. Fragment of one of the inscriptions pope Damasus had installed in the Domitilla catacomb. The inscription is recognizable as such because of the regularly shaped, classical lettering it contains.

de Rossi greatly influenced the way in which research was to be carried out by those who followed in their footsteps. This meant that henceforth only those scholars who would spend considerable amounts of time in the catacombs could expect to be taken seriously. At the same time, however, de Rossi's influence also resulted in the perpetuation of an approach to the catacombs in which archaeological research methods continued to be subordinate to considerations of more theological nature. It is no exaggeration to say that in the long run the approach as evidenced in the two greatest books ever to be written on the archaeology of the catacombs influenced the development of catacomb archaeology negatively. While other types of archaeology continued to develop into totally new directions as a result of the influence of the natural sciences, the study of catacomb archaeology did not keep up with these new developments, but instead long remained a static, and therefore and all too parochial affair, as we will now see.

## Recent Developments

The publication of de Rossi's work *Subterranean Christian Rome* triggered a whole new wave of research on the early Christian catacombs of Rome. Much of this research took the form of long and detailed catalogues through which scholars tried to make more readily available the enormous amounts of archaeological data preserved in the underground of the Roman Campagna. Thus, in 1922 began the publication of a series that contains a full rendering of all early Christian inscriptions ever found in the catacombs of Rome. This series, the publication of which continues to this very day, carries the title *Inscriptiones christianae urbis Romae VII saeculo anteriores* (*Christian Inscriptions from the City of Rome that Predate the Seventh Century A.D.*). It constitutes an almost inexhaustible source that informs us about the ideas and ideals of a significant portion of Rome's early Christian community. Other publications that fall into the category of the catalogue approach to catacomb archaeology comprise those in which early Christian wall paintings and early Christian sarcophagi have been documented through drawings and pictures as well as extensive descriptions. Considering the enormous amounts of artistic materials contained in these volumes, it may be evident that these studies have been an extremely important source of information for those interested in the genesis and development of early Christian art (fig. 11).

The publication of all these encyclopedic works of reference did not automatically mean, however, that the apologetic tendencies noted earlier vanished into thin air. It suffices to

Fig. 11. Famous representation of a fish with bread basket deriving from the Lucina region in the Callisto catacomb. Painted picture from Joseph Wilpert's 1903 monumental study of catacomb wall paintings.

go through Josef Wilpert's *Experiences and Results in the Service of Early Christian Archaeology. Retrospect of 45 Years of Scholarly Work in Rome* published in German in 1930. In this book, Wilpert, author of the wall painting and sarcophagus catalogues mentioned previously, freely attacked everyone about whose orthodoxy he, Wilpert, had doubts. Thus, in a discussion of research that had been carried out by one of his colleagues, Wilpert expressed his hope that this excellent piece of work would serve as example for "all those Christian scholars, and especially ecclesiastics, who switch off their piety in their study of religious topics for the sole purpose of wanting to pass themselves off as real scholars." To be sure, such remarks pale in comparison to what Wilpert had to say about Giacomo Boni, a noted Italian archaeologist and one of the excavators of the Forum Romanum. According to Wilpert – who writes that he received this information from a reliable source, which he then refrains from disclosing – Boni had discovered, in his excavations in the important sixth-century church of S. Maria Antiqua, a wall painting fragment with on it a representation of the head of Jesus. If we are to believe Wilpert, Boni took it, looked at it, and then threw it on the floor so that it broke into a thousand pieces. It hardly needs stressing that reports such as these tell us little about Wilpert's contemporaries and quite a lot about the manner in which Wilpert, no small scholar himself, led himself get carried away by the good old *jalousie de métier*.

The continued importance attached to arguments of an apologetic and theological nature, along with an approach that was essentially art historical and descriptive, explains why, in the early years of the twentieth century, catacomb archaeology did not keep up with developments that were transforming other kinds of archaeology. While many archaeologists now began to experiment with new excavation methods and were becoming aware of the ways in which the natural sciences could help them to unravel the past, archaeologists working in the catacombs were almost entirely oblivious to such trends, but instead preferred to carry on their research in exactly the same manner as de Rossi had done before them. Especially in the long run, the incapability or unwillingness to adopt new research methods was a development that was much to the detriment of catacomb archaeology. How important the application of such new research methods really is will become more apparent in Chapter II. There we will see that archaeologists working in the catacombs face a set of unique methodical problems – problems that can only be solved by an interdisciplinary approach in which there is no room for arguments of an apologetic or theological nature. That it was virtually impossible, incidentally, for catacomb archaeology to free itself from its Counter-reformist roots became evident, once more, in 1951, upon the publication of the excavations of an important pagan and early Christian necropolis located under St. Peter's in Rome. That publication engendered a rather lively discussion that focused not so much on the actual archaeological evidence that had been discovered or the field methods used to uncover it, but rather on the question of whether there was incontrovertible archaeological evidence to prove that the grave located right below the high altar of St. Peter's in Rome was in fact that in which Peter, the first Pope and founder of the Papacy, had originally been buried.

It was not until the 1970s that catacomb archaeology finally succeeded in freeing itself from traditions that had shaped this particular field of research for centuries. Only then, scholars began finally to apply the archaeological field methods the use of which had produced tangible results in other areas of archaeological research for more than half a century already. From that time onwards, new excavations were undertaken in the early Christian catacombs of Rome. Such excavations were no longer designed exclusively to gather information on the graves of the martyrs. Rather, their aim was to study these monuments in as comprehensive a fashion as possible in an attempt to reconstruct their building history on the basis of hard evidence. Through a careful examination of the complex networks of underground galleries, scholars finally succeeded, in the early 1980s, to reconstruct in a well-founded manner when and how the early Christian catacombs of Rome had come into existence (for details, see the next Chapter).

As soon as it began to dawn on scholars that early Christian art had not arisen in a historical or artistic vacuum, but rather that it should be seen against the background of trends that can also be discerned in the art produced by the Christian's non-Christian contemporaries, a lively discussion ensued on how to date the wall paintings that had been preserved in the catacombs of Rome in such impressive numbers. This discussion, which began in the 1960s, has still not been concluded. In fact, scholars now realize that their knowledge concerning the chronological development of wall painting in late antiquity rests, and continues to rest, on very shaky foundations indeed.

The most recent work in the catacombs is characterized by excavation projects during which all finds are being catalogued as completely and carefully as possible (fig. 12). While it was not unusual for past excavators to throw out all the pottery, for example, now such pottery is carefully inventoried, drawn and photographed. As a result of these developments, catacomb archaeology has finally, at the turn of the millennium, refined its research methods in such a fashion that its practitioners not longer need to be ashamed of the work they

are doing. There can be no doubt that in the near future this research will lead to new discoveries and that it will continue to produce new and exciting results. Such research will surely throw further light on a series of interesting questions concerning the origins of a religion that has shaped western civilization for the last two thousand years.

Fig. 12. Modern research in the catacombs of Rome.

# CHAPTER 2

# The Archaeology of the Catacombs

## Introduction

Catacombs are underground cemeteries that consist of intricate networks of subterranean galleries and burial chambers. The actual graves can be found everywhere in the catacombs, in the narrow galleries as well as in the more spacious burial chambers. Simple wall-graves are by far the most common. Such graves are rectangular in shape and may be found cut into the walls on both sides of the underground galleries. In the scholarly literature they are referred to as *loculi*. Other grave types include *arcosolia*-graves (graves surmounted by a semicircular arch) as well as sarcophagi (stone containers, literally "flesh-eaters"). Arcosolia and sarcophagi are usually, although not exclusively, found in burial chambers (the so-called *cubicula*).[1]

Even though catacombs occur in most countries around the Mediterranean, the Roman catacombs are by far the most famous and impressive. To date, some sixty catacombs have been discovered in the direct vicinity of this city. Some of these catacombs, such as the Callisto- and Domitilla-complexes, are truly underground "cities of the dead." Consisting of a network of corridors and burials chambers on five different levels, the galleries of the Callisto and Domitilla catacombs each extend under the surface for no less than 20 kilometers!

---

[1] Note, however, that loculi graves may sometimes be found in burial chambers and that arcosolia graves also occur along the underground galleries.

The term "catacomb" derives from the Greek. Originally it was used to indicate a spot on the Via Appia Antica near the present catacomb of Sebastian. In Antiquity, this spot was commonly referred to as "near the hollows" (*ad catacumbas*). These hollows had come into existence as a result of the quarrying that had been going on in this area long before the catacombs were built. When these quarries started to go out of use beginning in the second century A.D., people did not desert the places, but instead began to reuse these cavities, finding them appropriate spots to bury the dead. As time went on, these small underground burial complexes in the old quarries on the Via Appia continued to be used and enlarged so that an underground burial complex of considerable size was formed. This underground cemetery was referred to using the old topographical name already in use, namely "near the hollows." This usage continued for some time. In fact, throughout Antiquity, the term *the catacombs* (or hollows) remained closely linked to the site in question. Not until the Middle Ages did the term become a generic one. It was only from that time onwards that it could be used to indicate any type of large underground cemetery. To put it differently, it was only in the early Middle Ages that the term *catacomb* began to replace the term that until then had been commonly used to refer to what we now call the catacombs, namely the Latin *cryptae* (crypts). Today, scholars still use the term *catacomb* to denote large underground cemeteries. In addition, they also use the term *hypogeum* (literally "under the earth"), but they do so only to refer to underground burials complexes of smaller sites such as family vaults.

The Roman catacombs all have one thing in common: they have been carved out into tuff. Tuff is a volcanic rock that can be found everywhere in and around Rome. It derives from two volcanic areas, to the North and South of Rome respectively. Although the volcanoes in this area have ceased to be active long ago and have now become lakes – such as, for example, the Lago di Albano; the Lago di Nemi – they were very active in the period of 50,000 to 700,000 years ago. During that time they covered this part of central Italy with thick layers of volcanic materials (fig. 13).

In Antiquity, the Romans frequently used tuff for construction, for example to build walls such as the ones visible upon leaving Rome's central train station (Stazione Termini) or to produce the concrete Roman architects used to erect the proud and impressive structures that dot not only Rome, but other places in Rome's enormous Empire as well. From an architectural perspective, tuff offers all sorts of opportunities. On the one hand it has the advantage of being soft and can

Fig. 13. Rome as seen from the cupola of St. Peter's. In the background, the remains of vulcanoes that covered the Rome area with tuff, can be distinguished.

be quarried easily. On the other hand, tuff is strong enough to be used for construction purposes. These characteristics make tuff also ideal for the creation of underground galleries and cavities: while the tuff itself can be removed easily, the hollows that result from such an activity are stable enough to permit the creation of large underground spaces.

If one wants to gain a better understanding of the characteristics of tuff as well as of the techniques used to quarry it, the best thing to do is simply to visit the early Christian catacombs of Rome. There, on the tuff walls, it is possible, among other things, to discern the traces that have been left by the tools used by the original workmen (this can be accomplished by keeping a flashlight parallel against the wall). It hardly needs to be stressed that these traces have long interested archaeologists (fig. 14). Not only do such traces inform us about the tools that were used, but they also permit researchers to reconstruct the building history of individual galleries and, consequently, of entire catacombs (for details see

Fig. 14. Tuff wall in the catacombs. On the walls, the cutters' marks can still be seen. This wall was cut from left to right.

below). How soft the tuff of the catacombs can really be is apparent when one brushes one's hand lightly against the walls or ceilings of a gallery in the catacombs. By doing that one can feel that tuff has a sandy, grain-like structure. When one looks somewhat more carefully at the walls of galleries in their entirety, it is possible to notice that there exist various types of tuff that differ from one another in terms of color as well as structure or texture. These differences are important especially where it concerns the stability and hence the safety and usability of a layer: the grainier the tuff appears, the less stable a gallery dug into it will be. In Antiquity, people were keenly aware of these differences in consistency. This is evident from the unfinished galleries one can encounter in virtually every catacomb. Work in such galleries was abandoned because the original excavators were afraid that such a gallery might collapse as a result of the poor quality of the tuff upon which they had happened. Even though galleries have collapsed in the past, and will probably continue to do so in the future, it needs to be stressed, however, that at present there exists no imminent danger for visitors who frequent those parts of the catacombs that are open to the public. The Pontifical Commission for Sacred Archaeology – an organization that has been responsible for the early Christian catacombs of Rome for more than a century already – monitors the stability of the galleries that are open to the general public constantly.

## The Question of Dating and Chronology

In Chapter 1 we have seen than since their rediscovery in the sixteenth century, scholars have debated about the question of why and how the early Christian catacombs of Rome originated. The main reason why an earlier generation of scholars did not really find a satisfactory answer to this question is that these scholars did not succeed in dating the catacombs properly. That it is crucially important to establish a proper chronology for the catacombs becomes evident when one realizes that one first needs to know *when* the catacombs first came into being before one can begin to inspect the underlying social and religious forces that may have influenced this process. Inasmuch as such social and religious forces are never static but instead change constantly, and considering that there are considerable differences between the beliefs and practices of the first as opposed to, say, the third or fourth century A.D., it is imperative to establish during what period the catacombs were first excavated and to determine at what time they developed into large communal cemeteries.

In Chapter 1 it has been observed that for a long time scholars did not succeed in dating the catacombs because they did not really bother to investigate the question of the dating of the catacombs in any systematic fashion. Most scholars simply supposed that the catacombs in which the early Christian community of Rome laid to rest its dead had originated at the same time that this community had first come into being, namely in the course of the first century A.D. Such scholars hardly ever used archaeological evidence to support their contentions, but instead almost always arrived at an early dating of the catacombs by means of inference. Pointing out that the early Christian community of Rome had been obliged to bury its dead somewhere and being unable to locate early Christian cemeteries other than the catacombs, such scholars concluded that from the earliest beginnings of Christianity, Christians in Rome had invented catacombs for the interment of their co-religionists. Can such a conclusion be justified on the basis of the archaeological finds from the catacombs?

To answer this question properly, we first need to investigate the archaeological context from which these finds derive and to study some of the methodological problems scholars face in trying to establish the chronology of the catacombs.

From a methodological point of view, catacomb archaeology is different from all other kinds of archaeology in that the principle of stratigraphical excavations does not apply. Ever since archaeologists became aware of its importance, stratigraphy has been crucial in helping excavators to bring their digs to a successful conclusion. According to this principle, a site under excavation is viewed as a succession of layers (the Latin *stratum* means layer). The deeper a layer is located, the older (in terms of chronology) it is. By studying the layers sequentially, archaeologists are able to draw up a *relative* chronology; that is to say, they are able to determine which layer is older and which one more recent. By studying the archaeological materials preserved *in* the individual layers, archaeologists then try to "translate" this relative chronology into an *absolute* one, so that at the end of their excavation they are not only able to say which layers succeed one another, but also how much time elapsed before the remains associated with one layer went out of use before the remains associated with the next layer began to be utilized.

It is quite unfortunate that archaeologists who excavate in catacombs cannot generally use this stratigraphic guideline – the basis of modern archaeology. Catacombs consist of large networks of underground galleries that normally lack the kind of stratigraphic layering one encounters, for example, at an above-ground site that has been inhabited for several hundred years. Galleries in catacombs are only used once. In the catacombs construction always developed *horizontally* rather than vertically: after finishing one gallery and providing it with graves on all sides, workers would begin digging a new one at the end of the one they had just finished (fig. 15). For that reason, it is safe to assume that the further a gallery is

Fig. 15. Cross section of the burial room of Pope Cornelius in the Domitilla catacomb. Large air and light shafts (*lucernaria*) connected this room to the surface.

removed from the entrance of a catacomb, the more recent such a gallery must be. The traces left by the pickaxes of the workers permit us to determine in which direction such workers were heading and from which direction they were coming. It is by studying these traces that it becomes possible to determine how the different underground galleries developed sequentially. Thus it possible to establish a catacomb's *relative* chronology.

To translate this relative chronology into an *absolute* one is exceedingly difficult, however. In order to be able to say with confidence when exactly a gallery was excavated and used for burial, one needs datable archaeological finds. Unfortunately, more often than not, such datable finds are absent in the catacombs. Although it is true that the catacombs are replete with archaeological finds, it is also true that their value in terms of dating and chronology is, in many cases, extremely limited. There are two reasons why this is the case.

First of all, many finds are not found *in situ* (in their original location) but rather derive from a disturbed archaeological context. This is due to the fact that the catacombs have been open to visitors (including grave-robbers) for centuries. Until fairly recently, it was customary for such visitors to remove archaeological materials from their original location as they were searching the catacombs for antiquities they wanted to collect or sell.

A second complicating factor that often prevents us from arriving at a sound chronology for the catacombs is that those archaeological materials that do still remain *in situ* are often hard to date. It is true, for example, that the inscriptions one encounters almost everywhere in the catacombs can be dated on the basis of the names that occur in them or by studying the linguistic characteristics of the languages used in them, yet datings of this kind are not very precise. Something similar holds true for the wall paintings that have been preserved in the catacombs in quite impressive numbers. From the point of view of chronology, we still know very little about the development of wall painting in late antiquity. For a long time scholars assumed that it was possible to reconstruct the history of wall painting in late antiquity by studying the different pictorial styles in a comprehensive fashion. Discoveries in the Domitilla catacomb have indicated, however, that such an approach has its problems. In one of the cubicles of the Domitilla catacomb, two stylistically very different examples of wall painting were found painted next to one another on the very same wall. This implies that pictorial styles that differ in terms of formal appearance and usage of color can occur synchronically and concurrently, that is, not only at the same time, but also in the same place. The discovery in the Domtilla catacomb has made clear that dating on the basis of pictorial styles can therefore be a rather tricky affair. For that reason scholars now prefer to use more reliable evidence such as coins that can be found here and there in the catacombs and that can be dated with a great amount of precision (coins were not infrequently pressed into the wet stucco used to seal off graves). At times, inscriptions also carry absolute dates, unusually in the form of a reference to the city consuls (in ancient Rome, the year was dated by referring to the consuls that were in office that year; since we know the names of most of the consuls and we also know the year during which they were in office, it becomes possible to date very precisely inscriptions that carry the names of such consuls). Sometimes brick walls can be used for dating too, namely by comparing them with brick walls above ground (scholars have succeeded in dating brick walls by looking at their formal appearance; datings of this kind are usually not very precise, but they do at least give some indication of when a wall was constructed). Pottery can finally also be used for dating, even though, again, the value of such finds is more limited than is the case in regular excavations. The reason for this is simple: we still know very little about the history of pottery in late antiquity (fig. 16). In addition, in the

Fig. 16. Collection of late
antique pottery and lamp
fragments in the catacombs.

catacombs pottery has frequently not been preserved *in situ*,
but in a location other than where it had been placed originally.

Even though, therefore, it is true that even today it is frequently difficult to put a date on a particular gallery or grave,
it is also true that at present we know more about the
chronology of the catacombs than ever before. Just because
the present generation of scholars has studied the question
of when the catacombs originated more intensively than ever
before and just because they have tried to make use as
comprehensively as possible of the archaeological materials
discussed earlier, we are now in a position to reconstruct the
history of burial in the catacombs in a much more reliable
way than was possible, for example, in the days of Bosio or de
Rossi. Further research will help us, of course, to further
refine our knowledge of the chronology of the catacombs.
Still, such refinements are possible only because we already
dispose of a sound framework. Let us turn to this framework
to see what we really know about the genesis of the early
Christian catacombs of Rome.

## History and Development of the Early Christian Catacombs of Rome

The early Christian catacombs of Rome were not built in one day, but were constructed over a period of at least three centuries. They reflect the needs of a community that, especially in the late antique period, underwent considerable growth. On the basis of recent archaeological research, it is possible to distinguish four different phases in the history and development of the catacombs:

1. Phase during which the customs of underground burial originated (second and third centuries A.D.)
2. Phase during which the first real catacombs were constructed (third century A.D.)
3. Phase during which the catacombs developed into large underground communal cemeteries (fourth century A.D.)
4. Phase during which burial ceased; period of restoration and of visits by pilgrims (fifth through ninth century A.D.)

Although there are problems associated with the reconstruction of each individual phase, it should be stressed that the phase during which the catacombs originated is the one that is most difficult to reconstruct. The reason for this is as follows.

We have already seen that in the time of the Counter-reformation, scholars simply assumed that the catacombs had originated in the first century A.D. More recently, archaeologists have shown that nowhere in the catacombs does there exist archaeological materials that date to this early period. Quite the contrary. All archaeological materials that have been found in the catacombs date to the late second century A.D. at the earliest.

Such a state of affairs justifies the following two conclusions. First, lacking archaeological evidence dating to the first century, the early Christian catacombs of Rome did not originate in the first century but later, that is, at a time that Christianity had manifested itself in Rome for a considerable amount of time already, for at least a hundred years. Second, just because the catacombs did not yet exist in the first century, one must conclude that the early Christian community in Rome buried its dead in a place other than the catacombs.

Although the latter conclusion seems as inevitable as the former, it must be admitted that this conclusion raises other questions – questions that cannot be answered quite so easily. As soon as they began to realize that Rome's early Christian community buried in a "place other than the catacombs," scholars began to investigate where this place might have been and what it might have looked like. As they set out on their search, such scholars soon realized, however, that they were facing a rather tricky methodological problem. Inasmuch as Christian symbols and a Christian phraseology did not yet exist in this early period, they lacked the archaeological means to identify these early cemeteries. Even though they truly wanted to identify these early cemeteries and systematically looked for them, archaeologists thus realized that they would probably never be able to trace the beginnings of early Christian burial customs in Rome. The only approach left to them was the one that has gained widespread acceptance in scholarly circles, namely to hypothesize about these early burial places by studying the burial customs of a slightly later period and by then projecting these customs back into the period of the first century.

On the basis of such later evidence scholars now believe that the first Christians of Rome initially buried their dead in the same cemeteries and using the same burial customs as did their non-Christian neighbors. To support this hypothesis they cite the case of Martialis, who served as bishop in the Spanish town of Mérida (North of Cordoba) and of whom it is known that he had his sons interred in a pagan cemetery and according to local customs (around the middle of the third century A.D.). Although Martialis' act soon attracted the ire of his ecclesiastical colleagues, scholars are correct in stressing how interesting it is that such a thing could happen at all: apparently, Martialis, a (Christian) bishop, did not consider burying his sons on pagan land an inappropriate or unusual act – at least not until he was reprimanded. No less importantly, subsequent archaeological discoveries, especially in Rome, have shown that Martialis' behavior may have been more the rule than an exception. In Rome a considerable amount of archaeological evidence has survived that shows that the practice of using pagan cemeteries seems to have been fairly popular in Christian circles, even at a fairly late point in time. The Vatican necropolis provides us with a second and third century A.D. example of a pagan necropolis in which also Christians were laid to rest; the fourth century Via Latina catacomb with its impressive wall paintings in which pagan and early Christian imagery appears side by side provides an example of a still later period.

Such archaeological evidence is highly interesting. It shows that from a social point of view, the rise of Christianity must be considered as a very gradual process: in some families, certain members had converted to Christianity, while others had not. The archaeological evidence suggests quite strongly that despite such conversions, the family remained united in that it used the family grave to bury its deceased members, whether pagan or Christian. In light of such evidence, one can begin to understand why it is reasonable to suppose that the earliest Christian community in Rome whose remains we cannot trace archaeologically (as noted above) buried their dead in the same way as some of their co-religionists still did in the second, third, and fourth centuries, that is, in pagan necropoleis.

Before elaborating on why early Christian burial customs evolved in they way they did, it is necessary to consider some of the customs that were practiced in the pagan necropoleis we have just mentioned.

In the necropoleis of first century Rome, at a time that Christianity first began to manifest itself, the dead were interred only after they had been cremated. Their ashes were put into urns that were then placed in mausolea the impressive remains of which can be still be seen along the highways that connected Rome with her Empire (fig. 17). In the early second century A.D., however, cremation began to loose its appeal and slowly started to give way another burial custom, namely inhumation. The beginnings of this development can be dated to the reign of the emperor Hadrian (117-138 A.D.). There exists archaeological evidence that permits us to date the beginning of this change with a fair amount of precision. In the Vatican necropolis under St. Peter's, in the family graves that make up this cemetery, for example, one can still find several hypogea that contain, in one and the same hypogeum, small niches into which the ashes of the dead could be placed, and larger ones into which entire bodies could be interred.

Archaeologists as well as historians have long tried to determine why this shift happened, and why it happened at this time, yet none of the theories that have been formulated over the years has succeeded in convincing everyone. One thing is clear, however: the shift from cremation to inhumation had far-reaching consequences in terms of the space that

Fig. 17. Funerary complex of
Pomponius Hylas. The richly
decorated niches served as
containers for urns that
contained cremations.

was needed to provided people with a decent burial. As Romans who could afford it began to order large sarcophagi instead of small urns, such Romans also had to find the space needed to accommodate these enormous stone containers. Because the space available in the traditional mausolea was limited, it became customary in the course of the second century A.D. to expand such mausolea into the only direction into which expansion was still possible, namely, by going underground. Thus, the first underground hypogea that were constructed in this period were nothing but extensions of mausolea that were located on the surface. Not surprisingly, these early hypogea have in common that they are of limited extension and that they are accessible only via existing mausolea above ground.

One of the best examples of what happened has survived in an area that can be visited freely and that now forms part of the Sebastiano catacomb (fig. 18). The area comprises several traditional mausolea of which the one belonging to Clodius Hermes is the most famous. This mausoleum was built around A.D. 160 for a certain Clodius Hermes and his family – an extended family that included not only Clodius Hermes' relatives but also several of the family's *liberti* or freedmen. Although today the area is enclosed as a result of subsequent building activity at the site, the mausoleum of Clodius Hermes and the two other mausolea flanking it were originally located above ground, in the open air. Clodius Hermes' mausoleum is interesting in several respects. It contains not only urns for cremation, but also sarcophagi used for inhumation. It was such inhumations that led the owners of this family grave to commission the construction of a new burial chamber that is located on a lower level and that can be accessed via a staircase that connects the upper and lower floors. In the walls of the lower burial chamber eleven simple

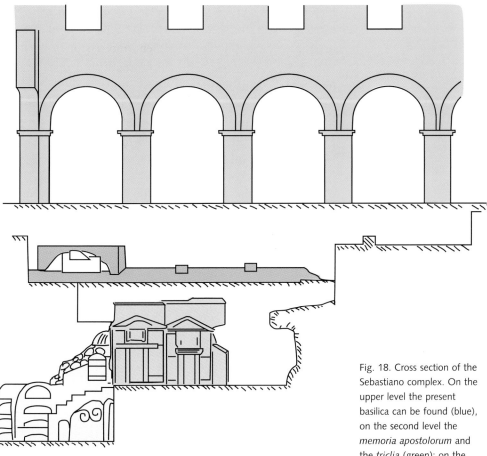

Fig. 18. Cross section of the Sebastiano complex. On the upper level the present basilica can be found (blue), on the second level the *memoria apostolorum* and the *triclia* (green); on the third level the Piazzuola with mausolea including that of Clodius Hermes (orange). These mausolea were constructed in an old quarry. These mausoleums were extended on a still lower level by means of hypogea (yellow).

graves were dug. They probably served to provide the freedmen of the family with an appropriate spot where their bodies could be interred in their entirety. Historically, the mausoleum of Clodius Hermes is a highly important monument in that it helps to document several things: the second century shift of cremation to inhumation; the beginnings of underground burial in the vicinity of Rome, also in the course of the second century A.D.; and the pagan origin of the custom of burying one's beloved ones underground.

It is crucially important to take the mentioned pagan roots into account if one wants to understand a phenomenon that may strike the innocent observer as an anomaly. Several subterranean burial chambers in Rome are decorated with wall paintings that are plainly pagan and that have little or nothing to do with Christianity at all. Some of these burial chambers can be found in small underground complexes. Others, however, can be found in the large early Christian catacombs of the city such as the Callisto and Sebastiano catacombs on the Via Appia Antica or the Domitilla catacomb on the Via Ardeatina. The reason why such pagan imagery occurs in early Christian catacombs is simple: all these paintings belong to underground family graves of the type of Clodius Hermes' mausoleum. As Christians began to excavate their catacombs in the same general areas where pagan families had buried for centuries and had provided their mausolea with underground extensions, it was only natural for workmen in the Christian catacombs to accidentally break into preexisting underground mausolea that abound in the area. Put differently, the cubicles with pagan imagery one sometimes encounters in the Christian catacombs of Rome were not originally part of these catacombs. Rather, they were preexisting structures that were integrated into the catacombs at a later point in time. Sometimes, but not always, such pagan hypogea were Christianized through the addition of early Christian iconographical motifs. This happened, for example, in one of the oldest parts of the Domtilla catacomb, in the so-called region of the Flavii (fig. 19). This region consists of a series of underground burial chambers dating to the late second century A.D.

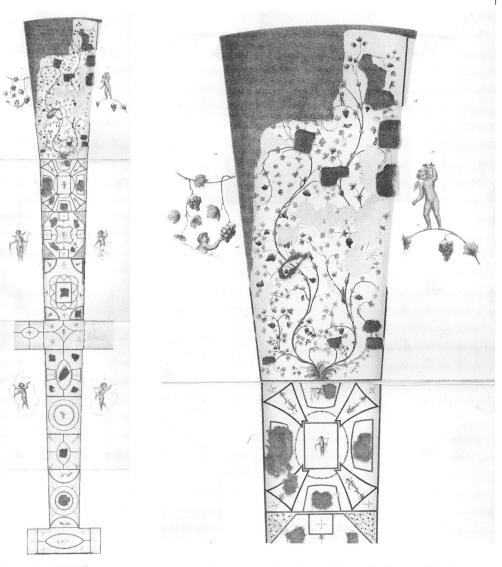

Fig. 19. Wall paintings on the ceiling of the so-called region of the Flavii, a long corridor that is now part of the Domitilla catacomb. The motifs document the popularity of bucolic and idyllic themes in second and third century wall paintings.

They were connected by means of a relatively broad gallery and were meant to accommodate sarcophagi. In the back of this gallery two rooms can be found that contain wall paintings that are unmistakably Christian, namely Daniel in the lion's den and Noah's ark. These paintings date to the third century A.D. – exactly the time that the pagan hypogeum was integrated into the Christian Domitilla catacomb.

As inhumation was becoming the most popular type of burial in late Roman society at large in the late second and early third century, the need to find the necessary space to bury the dead appropriately became ever more pressing. With an estimated population of around one million people, and, moreover, being a home to men and women whose life expectancy was comparable to that of people in the less developed countries today, Rome was facing a problem that was becoming more serious every year: where should all these people be buried?

The initial response to this problem was the one we have already encountered: open-air mausolea were given underground extensions. As these underground extensions became more customary in Rome's crowded necropoleis, it was not unusual for workers to "bump into" other underground extensions in the area. This explains the apparent irregularity in the plans of some catacombs. Such irregularity was not the result of a particular way of planning the catacombs. Rather, such irregularity is due to the fact that the areas in question are the result of a series of uncoordinated individual efforts to expand below ground. The areas in question cannot really be considered as real catacombs. They are rather collections of interconnected hypogea, that is, of burial chambers that had originally been planned as separate underground units. A good example of the integration of several originally independent hypogea can be found in the catacomb of Vibia (fig. 20).

The custom of underground burial as it arose in second-century Rome stands at the beginning of a development that would soon lead, in the course of the third century, to the construction of underground cemeteries that were designed as such from the very start. The contemporaneous emergence of early Christian art – that is, imagery that is typically Christian from an iconographic perspective – allows us, moreover, to determine the role Christians played in this process. The existence of such Christian imagery permits us to conclude that the pagan custom of extending one's mausoleum underground by means of one or more burial chambers seems to have enjoyed popularity in Christian circles as well. In the course of the third century A.D., several underground

Fig. 20. Wall painting from the Vibia catacomb, illustrating a funerary banquet that takes place in an otherworldly setting. Vibia can be seen on the left as she is led into this paradise setting.

hypogea were excavated in the vicinity of Rome that in terms of formal appearance look exactly like the pagan ones, but that have to be identified as Christian on the basis of the imagery and inscriptions they contain.

At this time there was still another development that merits our attention and that seems to have been limited to Christian circles only. In addition to using hypogea that clearly stand in the tradition of the pagan underground extensions, Christians began to construct underground cemeteries that were specifically and from the beginning designed as such. Such cemeteries differed from those connected to a pre-existing mausoleum in several ways: they could be entered immediately, via one or more staircases; they consisted of a network of underground galleries and were designed specifically to offer as much space as possible for inhumation; they were also constructed in such a way that the excavation of new or additional underground galleries could be done with the least amount of effort. It is in this respect in particular that these cemeteries differ from the mausolea that preceded them: these were large underground necropoleis in which an entire community and not just individual families could be laid to rest.

Recent archaeological research has shown that the builders of these "wholly-underground" cemeteries or catacombs frequently used old quarries or cisterns as a starting point. Famous examples of this can be found in the Sebastiano catacomb on the Via Appia where an old sand quarry (*arenarium*) was used for this purpose, and in the Priscilla catacomb on the Via Salaria, where an old underground network of cisterns of water tunnels was transformed into an early Christian catacomb (fig. 21). That these were originally water tunnels is still evident today: these tunnels differ from regular catacomb galleries in size (they are broader than galleries one usually encounters in the catacombs), shape (their ceiling is more rounded), and floor level (not horizontal but sloping so as to let the water flow into one direction).

That the developments we have described should not merely be seen as a response to changing burial customs, and the lack of space that resulted from it, becomes evident when we turn to the literary sources. Such sources tell us that there were other factors that contributed to this process. We know that in the early third century A.D. Pope Zepherynus (195-217 A.D.) appointed his deacon Calixtus as overseer of a subterranean cemetery that specifically served to bury the poorest members of Rome's early Christian community (the catacomb in question is called Callisto catacomb on the Via Appia Antica; Calixtus himself was buried in the Calepodio catacomb on the Via Aurelia). Archaeologists have identified the

Fig. 21. Water channel in the Torlonia catacomb.
This channel is recognizable as such on the basis of the gallery's curved ceiling, the sloping floor level, as well as the lack of tombs.

area for which Calixtus was responsible: it is the so-called Area I in the Callisto catacomb (fig. 22). This Area I can still be visited today (it is near the "crypt of the popes," see Chapter 1). It consists of two parallel galleries that are connected to one another by a series of additional galleries, all of which

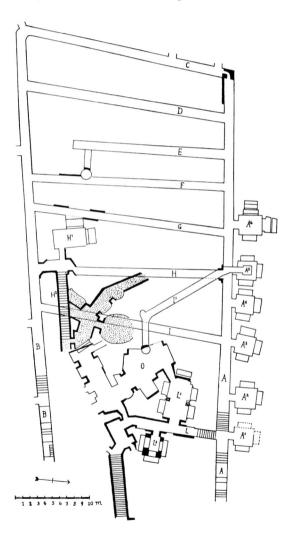

Fig. 22. The so-called Area I in the Callisto catacomb. Archaeologists have identified this area as the place where Calixtus installed his cemetery for the poor.

contain simple graves. The Area I is a prime example of rational planning, and of a cemetery that was designed from the very start as a communal burial ground where people could be buried together and in great numbers.

Our sources also indicate that the people who were buried in the Area I only had to cover the costs of the funeral undertaker; all other expenses, such as the construction of the underground galleries and the cutting of the graves, were covered by the church. With such measures, the early Christian community of Rome laid the basis for a development that would lead, especially in the course of the fourth century A.D., to the construction of large underground Christian catacombs. It was exactly because the early Church took on the responsibility for the construction of (underground) cemeteries in which only Christians were to be buried that Rome's early Christian community distinguished itself from other groups. That this is so follows from the writings of contemporary, non-Christian writers. They identify the care with which Christians regarded the poor and the dead as something typically Christian and as something they themselves found hard to understand if not impossible to fathom.

## Rise and Decline of the Roman Catacombs

We have just seen how, in the course of the third century A.D., Rome's early Christian community began to excavate ever-larger underground cemeteries that were specifically designed to bury large numbers of people in big communal cemeteries. This usage was continued in the fourth century. It was only then, at a time that Christianity could develop freely, that the catacombs were turned into the huge underground cemeteries that we know today. In fact, two thirds of the entire network of underground galleries in Rome's catacombs can be dated to this period. Scholars have hypothesized that a total of 750.000 graves can be found in the catacombs, but lacking reliable research on this issue, this figure must for now be regarded as speculative.

It is more than likely that during the fourth century the church administered the early Christian catacombs of Rome in the same way, as had been the case in the Callisto catacomb in the early third century. As Christianity was coming of age, Rome had been divided in seven administrative ecclesiastical districts. These districts were subdivided, in turn, into parishes. People belonging to one parish were usually – although not always – buried in the catacomb that belonged to the ecclesiastical district of which their parish was part. Thus, for example, people who went to church in the Santa Sabina on the Aventine were buried in the Comodilla catacomb on the Via Ostiense because this was the catacomb that belonged to the district to which the Santa Sabina parish belonged.

The actual work in the catacombs was carried out by *fossores*. Such *fossores* were not only responsible for burying the dead, but also for digging graves and for constructing the underground galleries that could accommodate the graves. In several catacombs, representations of such *fossores* while at work have been preserved. In the case of the Domitilla catacomb, we even know the name of the *fossor* represented on the walls of an arcosolium there: he was called Diogenes (fig. 23). As is evident from these representations, *fossores* were men who had to work hard and under unfavorable conditions, using oil lamps and pickaxes to assist them with their tiresome job. At first, *fossores* received payment from church officials. Later, in the course of the fourth and fifth centuries, *fossores* began operating as independent entrepreneurs. This is evident from inscriptions that indicate how these people made money by selling graves. From the sixth century

onwards, the *fossores* began to play a less prominent role. As burial in the catacombs was becoming increasingly unusual, they lost their *raison d'être* and were replaced by church officials who were henceforth responsible for the maintenance and for restoration work in the catacombs.

With the rapid growth of the Christian community in Rome in the fourth century, the catacombs were soon too small to accommodate the thousands of new believers that needed to find a resting place in these subterranean cemeteries. Using excavation techniques that had been developed in the third century, engineers and *fossores* were now facing the task of constructing large underground cemeteries that could accommodate thousands of people. To accomplish it, rational thinking and careful planning was necessary.

Fig. 23. Wall painting from the Domitilla catacomb, containing a rendering of the *fossor* Diogenes. Even though this painting is partially destroyed, the shovel (*dolabra*) that Diogenes used to cut the galleries of this catacomb can still be discerned.

The catacombs that were constructed during this period show how the ancient engineers solved the problem they were facing: the layout of galleries as well as the layout of the graves that were cut into the walls of these galleries was done systematically according to a preset plan. A look at any map of a catacomb dating to this period makes clear what happened. Such maps indicate that the irregular galleries that characterize the catacombs of the third century were then a thing of the past. The catacombs of the fourth century all have regular plans. Galleries run in remarkably straight lines. When galleries cross other galleries, they do so at right angles. In some catacombs, a pattern of underground galleries emerges that scholars refer to as "fishbone" (looking like a fishbone, this pattern consists of a straight main gallery from which other galleries depart to the left and right, at regular intervals). Regularity also reigns supreme where it concerns the arrangement of the graves. While in catacombs dating to the third century, it was customary to find loculi that are dispersed over the entire wall of the gallery, galleries dating to the fourth century never display such an uneconomic use of space: here the loculi are arranged in regular piles of four to eight graves on top of one another, covering the entire wall. Even where galleries meet and the walls needed to be strong to support the vaults of the crossing galleries, wall space was used as economically as possible, namely through the cutting of small size loculi that could accommodate children.

As people were buried massively in the catacombs and burial there became the standard mode of burial starting in the fourth century, it also became fashionable for the rich to use these underground cemeteries. This explains why it is only from this period onwards that we encounter in the catacombs of Rome not only just simple graves, but also richly decorated ones, such as beautifully painted *arcosolia* and

richly refurbished *cubicula*. The presence of such richly decorated graves and burial chambers is important because it is
precisely these paintings that permit is to reconstruct the genesis and early history of early Christian wall painting (fig. 24).

The expansion of the catacombs in the fourth century
finally also explains why most inscriptions from the catacombs date to this period as well. To date, some 40,000
inscriptions have been discovered in the early Christian catacombs. Such inscriptions served to mark the graves of the
dead and to commemorate the deeds of the person or persons
buried there. A special class of inscriptions is formed by those
that refer to martyrs, Christians who had died during the
great anti-Christian persecutions of the third and early fourth
century. In the course of the fourth century, the graves of the
martyrs were embellished on papal instigation. In the course
of such embellishments, graves that had originally been quite
simple were turned into ostentatious shrines that soon began
to attract believers, not just from Rome, but from all over
Europe.

Fig. 24. Richly decorated
burial chamber in the Vigna
Randanini catacomb,
containing a wall grave
(*loculus*) on the wall's upper
register and an arched grave
(*arcosolium*) on the wall's
lower side.

It is still unclear whether burial in the catacombs continued in the fifth and sixth century A.D. In the Sebastiano catacomb a grave inscription has survived that can be dated to the year A.D. 535, yet it seems rather unlikely to suppose that by this time the catacombs were still used for burial on a large scale. The following factors contributed to the decline of burial in the catacombs at this time: a general decline in population whereby the total number of 800,000 inhabitants that still lived in Rome in the early fifth century had been reduced to a mere 100,000 in the early sixth; the unstable political situation that resulted in Rome being replaced as capital of the Empire by Constantinople; a series of sieges that began with Alaric's siege of A.D. 410 – clearly a period during which the catacombs could not be used for burial and when many graves in the catacombs were broken into; and, finally, the emergence of a new burial custom as a result of which people stopped burying their dead underground and outside the city, but inside the city, in open air cemeteries.

From the fifth through the ninth centuries, the catacombs were not forgotten, but they no longer served as cemeteries. People still visited them, but only to see and pray at the graves of the martyrs. Such people did not only include the local population, but also those that traveled to Rome from all over Europe for the specific purpose of visiting the matyrial graves and subterranean sanctuaries of the catacombs. The *itineraria* we discussed in Chapter 1 were written during this period. Such pilgrimages continued well into the ninth century. They ceased when church authorities began unearthing the bones of the martyrs to transport and rebury them in churches that were located inside the city of Rome. Once the remains of martyrs had been removed from the catacombs, people so began to forget about these early Christian "cities of the dead." Until their rediscovery in the time of the

Counterreformation, for more than six hundred years, the early Christian catacombs of Rome would disappear from public view.

## The Graves of the Martyrs in the Catacombs

When Christianity first began to manifest itself, its adherents frequently found themselves facing authorities who were not very receptive of this newly-founded religion and who often believed that Christianity ought to be destroyed by fire and sword. Especially during the reigns of the Emperor Decius, around the middle of the third century, and the Emperor Diocletian, in the beginning of the fourth century, this view resulted in more or less systematic persecutions during which many Christians died violent deaths. Such Christians, whose steadfastness impressed both their Christian and non-Christian contemporaries greatly, were known as martyrs or witnesses (the Greek word *martyr* means witness). Because of their willingness to die for their beliefs, martyrs were seen as courageous imitators of Jesus. Like Jesus who had given up his life to free the world of sin, martyrs also were not afraid to bring the highest sacrifice possible.

As time went on and the memory of the great anti-Christian persecutions of previous centuries began to fade, Christians did not forget the martyrs of old. Beginning in the fourth century, martyrs were increasingly regarded in Christian circles as people whose main role in the religious life of the early Christian community was that of heavenly go-between. Following a passage in the Revelation of John (6:9-11), Christians believed that martyrs rested "under the altar," that is, in the direct vicinity of God. They also believed that because of this resting place, martyrs were in the best possible position to intercede with God on their behalf. In this period such intercessions were deemed desirable because people thought that when they died they would not go to heaven immediately (as martyrs did), but instead would have to wait for a considerable amount of time until their bodies had been cleansed and their souls purified. It was during this period of post-mortem cleansing and purification, when body and soul were separated, that martyrs could help the dead prepare for the Last Judgement and the Resurrection of the Dead.

The archaeological evidence that has survived in the catacombs of Rome provides us with excellent examples of early Christianity's respect for the martyrs. Just because martyrs were seen as people who could influence the post-mortem fate of those who had passed away, it was only natural that people wanted to be buried as closely to a martyr's grave as possible (fig. 25). In almost all early Christian catacombs of Rome one encounters ample evidence documenting the popularity of

Fig. 25. Cross section of the grave of Pope Cornelius in the Callisto catacomb with *ossuarium* that served to bury large groups of people in the proximity of this pope, who later became a saint.

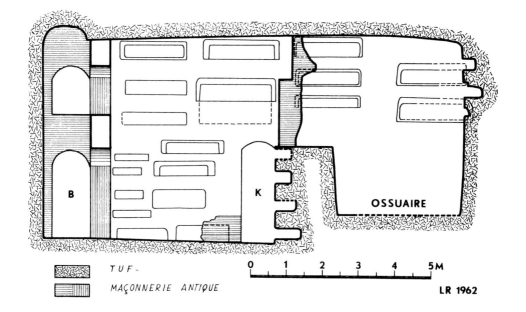

this custom. In fact, in any area where the density of graves is high, one can be sure that the area includes the grave of at least one early Christian martyr. Although tombs located near a martyr's grave often strike the modern visitor as unimpressive, it is important to recall that despite their simple appearance, such graves were occupying the most prominent spot, and therefore the most desirable spot in an entire catacomb. Thus, such graves were places where only people with enough distinction or money could hope to find a free spot. Graves of this type occur in areas that are denoted with the term *retro sanctos* (literally "behind the holy ones"). The location of graves in *retro sanctos* areas, namely in the direct vicinity, explains why this term was used. The meaning of mentioned term is especially appropriate in case of the evidence preserved in the Domitilla catacomb. There, in the area directly behind the apse of the basilica of the Saints Nereus and Achilleus, a series of richly decorated burial chambers can be found that date to the fourth century. There can be little doubt that these burial chambers belonged to wealthy families. They were constructed here for the specific purpose of creating final resting places for the rich who had the advantage of being in direct proximity to the graves of these saints. It is perhaps not by accident that in one of the wall paintings that have survived in this part of the catacomb, one encounters an illustration of how the role martyrs were believed to play was conceived. On the back wall of an arcosolium we see a representation of the woman who was buried here. Her name was Veneranda. Veneranda is not alone, however. On the painting also appears a certain Petronilla. She was a martyr, and believed to be the daughter of Peter. On the painting Petronilla can be seen leading Veneranda into Paradise (fig. 26). Thus the painting illustrates how those who commissioned it viewed Pentronilla's function, namely, as heavenly patron who would

Fig. 26. Wall painting in the Domitilla catacomb with a representation of Veneranda – the dead person who is buried here – who is being led into paradise by Saint Petronilla.

take care of Veneranda from the moment she slipped away from her mortal existence on this earth.

Still another good example testifying to the popularity of being buried near the martyrs, *retro sanctos* can also be observed in the "crypt of the popes" in the Callisto catacomb. Since popes were believed to be similar to martyrs in that they too were credited with the capability of intervening with God to influence the fate of the common dead, people were desirous to be buried close to the graves in which the mortal remains of such holy fathers had been laid to rest. In the case of the Callisto catacomb, the wish to bury people near the "crypt of the popes" resulted in a lack of space that became more pressing as time went on. In due course, additional space was created by removing the bones of the common dead (not the popes!) from their graves and depositing them in an enormous communal grave or *ossuarium* that was located directly behind the "crypt of the popes." This enormous bone-container could accommodate the remains of hundreds of people.

Although private initiatives played a considerable role in the fourth-century cult surrounding the graves of the martyrs, it would not be entirely correct to assume that this cult flourished exclusively as a result of such initiatives. Quite the contrary. Church officials were interested in the cult of the martyrs too, and beginning in the fourth century, they did everything in their power to further this cult in ways that were congenial to early Christian theology and Church policy. This explains, among other things, why many of the famous fourth-century basilicas that can be found on the outskirts of the city of Rome are located on top of catacombs in which martyrs were buried to whose memory these basilicas are dedicated. This is the case, for example, with St. Peter's, with the church of the Holy Agnes on the Via Nomentana, with the basilica of Saint Laurence outside the Walls on the Via Tiburtina, with the church of the Saints Peter and Marcellinus on the Via Casilina, as well as the Basilica Apostolorum (also called church of Saint Sebastian) on the Via Appia Antica. The basilica of the Saints Nereus and Achilleus that forms an integral part of the Domtilla catacomb complex also falls into this category.

Of all popes interested in commemorating the martyrs, Pope Damasus (A.D. 366-384) stands out. During his pontificate, his collaborators drew up an inventory of where in the catacombs the graves of martyrs were located. Such an inventory was useful because by this time it was not unusual that the exact original location of a martyr's grave had been forgotten. Until large-scale commemorations of their tombs began in the course of the fourth century, martyrial graves did not generally differ (in terms of physical appearance) from the other graves that could be found in the catacombs. They were mostly simple graves, in some cases carrying a short inscription or some sort of simple decoration.

Under Damasus, all of this changed rather dramatically. The graves of martyrs were now embellished, thus attracting the attention of everyone who entered the catacombs. In some cases, altars were installed next to a martyr's grave so that the Eucharist could be celebrated there. This was important, especially because it provided believers with an appropriate architectural setting to commemorate, in the appropriate liturgical fashion, the day that the martyr in question had originally died or, rather, "received the crown of martyrdom." Pope Damasus also had the tombs of the martyrs embellished by means of long funerary inscriptions, that is, elegant pieces of stone that carried funerary epigrams that Damasus himself composed. Evoking the life and sufferings of the martyrs, such inscriptions were meant to inspire compassion in those who read them and to make sure that their deeds would never be forgotten.

To date, the remains of about 80 of such funerary inscriptions have been discovered. A beautiful example can be found, for example, in the "crypt of the popes" in the Callisto catacomb (this is the famous inscription de Rossi rediscovered in the mid nineteenth century, see chapter 1). Inscriptions of this type are easily recognizable because of the lettering that appears in them. Being classical or very regular in appearance, the letters in these inscriptions are the work of a certain Furius Dionysius Filocalus. It is rather extraordinary that we should know this man's name at all. In Antiquity, workmen such as Furius Dionysius Filocalus were not generally held in high esteem. Consequently, hardly ever have their names been transmitted to posterity. The case of Furius Dionysius Filocalus is different, however. This stone-carver was a self-conscious man who took pride in his work and who "signed" several of this inscriptions he made using the phrase "Furius Dionysius Filocalus made it."

The inscriptions erected by Damasus are interesting in a number of other respects too. Most importantly, they contain information that cannot be found in any other source. A good example of the style and type of information these inscriptions contain can be found in an epitaph Damasus composed to commemorate one of his predecessors, pope Eusebius: "Bishop Damasus made it. Heraclius forbade the unfaithful to do penance; Eusebius on the other hand taught those poor fellows how to lament one's own sins. The people divided into two parties; anger increased all the time. Disturbances, murder, war, dissension, struggles. Instantly both are banned by the cruel tyrant, even though the bishop had done his best to preserve the peace. Cheerfully, by the will of God, he accepts his exile. On Sicily he leaves this world and dies. To Eusebius, bishop, martyr."

Damasus' work in the catacombs soon led to a renewed interest in everything that had to do with the martyrs and their graves. Christians from all over Europe began to flock to Rome where they visited the catacombs in ever-larger numbers. As the number of visitors to the catacombs in general and to the graves of the martyrs in particular increased, the necessity presented itself to make these sites accessible for large groups of people. This led to yet another round of construction work around the graves of the martyrs. In addition to enormous shafts, constructed in such a way as to permit air and light to stream into the subterranean galleries of the catacombs, large staircases were now constructed. Such staircases enabled visitors to enter in large numbers. They also help to direct the stream of people in the often cramped underground setting of the catacombs (in some catacombs there was one staircase for people entering a specific area, and another for those exiting it).

There can be little doubt that a visit to the graves of the martyrs impressed the early medieval visitors to the catacombs greatly. Many of these visitors left graffiti in which they expressed, often in a somewhat rudimentary form, their feelings and beliefs. Some pilgrims just left their names, others invoked the names of the martyrs buried there. Still others left short exclamatory notes. As space was limited, it was not unusual for visitors to scribble their messages on top of one another, as a result of which deciphering such graffiti is sometimes extremely difficult. A good example of what graffiti left by pilgrims and visitors looks like can be found in the Sebastiano catacomb. There an entire wall of graffiti has been preserved (now behind glass).

A visit to the graves of the martyrs offered visitors not just an opportunity to pray, but also the opportunity to physically touch these graves. This was important because Christians believed that holiness was transferrable through physical contact. Not infrequently, visitors to the catacombs would lay cloth on the graves of martyrs, or they would pour oil onto it which they then took with them upon returning to their country of origin. There, such cloth and oil bottles were kept as relics. Because such relics were holy in the most tangible sense, they could used for a variety of purposes. Just as relics could help to cure the sick, they could also be used to settle disputes that were essentially social or political in nature. Through such relics, early Christian martyrs whose remains were buried in the catacombs of Rome succeeded in attaining fame all over Europe.

The custom of visiting the graves of the martyrs continued well into the Middle Ages, until Pope Paschalis I (757-767) and some of his successors started to remove the mortal remains of the martyrs from the catacombs. As soon as these martyrial remains could no longer be found in the catacombs, the catacombs began to loose their appeal. Now that these remains had been reburied in various churches in Rome itself, a visit to the catacombs became superfluous. Once this process of transferal that had started under Paschalis I had been completed in the ninth century, the catacombs ceased to attract attention. Interest in the catacombs did not revive until the late sixteenth century. Only then did people realize how intriguing these subterranean cemeteries really are and how much art has been preserved in them. Let us now turn to a discussion of these artistic remains in the catacombs of Rome.

# CHAPTER 3

# The Art of the Catacombs

## Introduction

Many works of art have been preserved in the early Christian catacombs of Rome. Such works of art form the single most important source of information concerning the genesis and the earliest history of early Christian art. That early Christian works of art have survived in the catacombs so well and in such astonishing quantities can be attributed to the following factors. First of all, the catacombs have always provided an excellent setting for such works of art to survive the ravishes of time. Unlike other settings in which works of art are exposed to the detrimental influences of environmental factors, the setting provided by the catacombs is a much more stable one. Throughout the ages there was little climatic change in the catacombs. Moreover, hardly any building activity took place there after the catacombs went out of use, thus minimizing the chance that wall paintings and other works of art were ruined as a result of such activities.

How fortunate it really is that such conditions apply becomes evident when one realizes that the catacombs constitute, in and by themselves, true treasure houses of art. This was a natural consequence of the fact that the catacombs were constructed for the specific purpose of providing many thousands of people with a spot where they could be buried properly. Given that purpose, it was inevitable for the catacombs to attract scores of artisans who embellished the graves of many of those who rested here. Thus, as more and more people were buried in the long and winding galleries of the catacombs, these "cities of the dead" soon became to assume the character of "picture-galleries."

Recent advances in the study of the archaeology of the cat-acombs have helped scholars in their attempts to reconstruct how early Christian art first came into existence. More specifically, new insights regarding the dating of the catacombs (see Chapter 2) have helped to create a chronological framework that permits scholars to study the earliest history of early Christian art in a more systematic fashion than ever before. As a result of such advances, we now know that early Christian art did not come into existence overnight, but rather it developed gradually and as part of artistic trends that can also be discerned in circles other than Christian. To study this evolutionary process is interesting because such an investigation permits us to learn more about the history of the early Christian community in Rome (fig. 27).

Fig. 27. Monumental portrait bust of Constantine in the courtyard of the Palazzo dei Conservatori in Rome.

It is customary for scholars who study the history of early Christian art to distinguish between a *technical*, a *stylistic*, and an *iconographic* approach. Such a distinction allows scholars to analyze in depth the various factors that play a role in the development of early Christian art. As a result of this approach, we now know that from a technical and stylistic point of view, early Christian art did not differ very much from other contemporary, non-Christian art forms. We also know, however, that insofar as the themes represented were concerned, early Christian art soon began to distinguish itself from the iconography that was common in the ancient world. In the course of this process, motifs taken from classical mythology were replaced by themes taken from the Bible, with special emphasis on themes taken from the New Testament. Evidence for such a development becomes especially tangible from the fourth century onwards.

The iconographic approach has permitted scholars to distinguish three separate phases in the development of early Christian art as preserved in the catacombs of Rome. They include:

1. The earliest phase (the genesis of early Christian art; second and third centuries A.D.)
2. The Old Testament phase (third century A.D.)
3. The New Testament phase (fourth and fifth centuries A.D.)

In the pages that follow we will discuss these phases at some length. This discussion will provide us with the necessary framework to explore why early Christian art developed in the way it did. In the course of this discussion it will also become clear in what ways an investigation of the stylistic and technical aspects can help us to better understand the genesis of early Christian art in its relationship to contemporary pagan art.

## The Genesis of Early Christian Art and the Old Testament Phase

In Chapter 2 we have seen how, initially, Rome's early Christian community participated in funerary customs that were not specifically Christian. We have also seen that Christian cemeteries that were designed as such from the start did not come into existence until the early third century A.D. Something similar applies for early Christian art. Early Christian art was not born in one day. Rather, it took time for an early Christian iconography to develop. When a typically early Christian iconography finally appeared, it was the result of a long and gradual process. Study of this process is interesting, because it enables us to learn more about early Christian attitudes, not only towards art, but also towards contemporary society in general as well.

When Christianity first appeared on the scene, there was no Christian art. At that time, Christians who were interested in objects of an artistic nature had two options from which to choose: they could either use objects that were currently available or, alternatively, they could begin to develop an iconography that was appropriate within the context of their religious ideals and sensibilities. As we will see in a moment, it was this latter option that led to the emergence of early Christian art as we know it. Yet, it was due to the popularity gained by the first option that a framework was created that enabled the second option to come to fruition. Let me explain.

Art historical research has shown that when Christianity first began to manifest itself, Christians made use of objects that were commonly available. Such objects displayed an iconography that had nothing to do with Christianity. For that reason, such objects can be recognized as having been used by Christians only in exceptional cases. A good (and rare) example of such an object has survived in the form of a sarcophagus that was used to bury a certain Marcus Aurelius Prosenes. This sarcophagus, the impressive remains of which can be found in the gardens of the Villa Borghese, is a large marble container that belongs to a category of sarcophagi that enjoyed enormous popularity in the third century in non-Christian circles (fig. 28). As was usual on Roman sarcophagi, the decoration of this piece could be found on the front. It consists of richly sculpted festoons, putti, and cornucopias – evidently all themes that are not specifically Christian. On the sarcophagus' lid Prosenes has been represented in a three-dimensional fashion (his head has been lost). On the basis of the inscription on the front side of the sarcophagus, we know that Prosenes was no nobody: he served as superintendent in the palace of the emperor Commodus (A.D. 180-192). In that capacity he was responsible for administrative and financial matters, including the supervision of the imperial wine cellar and the organization of gladiatorial games.

That Prosenes converted to Christianity follows from a second, much less impressive inscription that was carved on

Fig. 28. Front side of the sarcophagus of Marcus Aurelius Prosenes. Putti carry the inscription that contains a description of Prosenes' career.

the upper right side of the sarcophagus. According to this inscription, on March 3 of the year A.D. 217, Prosenes was "led back to God." On the basis of this inscription we know what we could never have known on the basis of the iconography of the sarcophagus alone, namely that Prosenes was not merely an important official, but someone who had converted to Christianity as well.

It may be obvious that the evidence provided by the sarcophagus of Prosenes is very interesting from a methodological point of view. This evidence not only suggests that Christians used what was commonly available. It also suggests that if the inscription had not been added and preserved, we would have had no way at all of knowing that a convert to Christianity used this sarcophagus. The implication of these observations may be clear. If it is true that at first Christians used the same *objets d'art* as everybody else, then it is impossible for us, at least in most cases, to recognize these objects as such. Put differently, just because we cannot recognize these objects as having used by Christians, we will never be able to determine how popular such usage may have been.

From a modern perspective, it may seem strange that Christians would have used objects the iconography of which is plainly pagan, or at least neutral, instead of Christian. Still, the surviving evidence suggests the earliest Christian communities did not find this practice unacceptable. It was only as time went by and Christianity began to develop into a major religious movement, that Christians began to feel the need for an iconography that would express their system of belief in ways that were not possible using current iconographic schemata. On the basis of a passage in the writings of the Church Father Clement of Alexandria (lived A.D. 160-215), we know that Christians were permitted to use *objects d'art* produced in pagan workshops, but that, at the same time, were also advised to choose only those objects that were decorated with motifs that were appropriate from a Christian point of view. In the passage in question, Clement writes that Christians are permitted to wear signet finger rings made in pagan workshops for one reason in particular, namely because such rings could serve a practical purpose, namely as seals to mark off one's property. According to Clement, the following motifs are appropriate: the dove, fish, a ship, a lyre, an anchor, and a fisherman. Such motifs, although clearly of pagan derivation, were deemed appropriate because each of them could be interpreted as referring to notions that were specifically Christian.

Archaeological evidence, and engraved inscriptions in particular, indicate that the iconographic motifs sanctioned by Clement soon began to enjoy popularity in Christian circles outside Alexandria too. A good example can be found in the Museo Nazionale Romano (Thermae Museum). It is a funerary inscription that dates to the third century and derives from the Vatican necropolis (fig. 29). In the inscription, two fish can be discerned that flank an anchor. Above this representation an inscription has been carved that reads *ichthus zoontoon. Ichthus* is the Greek word for fish; *zoontoon* means "of the living." The exact meaning of this phrase becomes evident when one realizes that the term *ichthus* is not just a Greek word, but an acronym. It is an abbreviation of the phrase "Jesus Christ God's Son Savior (*Ie̅sos Ch̅ristos T̅heou H̅uios S̅oter*). In the case of the inscription under discussion, Jesus is therefore the savior of the living – a concept that also is expressed visually by means of the fish and the anchor carved below mentioned inscription. In early Christian art, the anchor symbolizes hope. This association derives from a passage in the New Testament where such an association is explicitly made (namely Hebrews 6:19).

The adaptation by Christians of iconographic themes that were common in the ancient world also applies for motifs not mentioned by Clement. Of these, the *kriophoros* is the most frequently occurring theme (fig. 30). *Kriophoros* is Greek and means ram bearer. It is an iconographical type that enjoyed great popularity in the ancient world from the moment it was first introduced beginning in the seventh century B.C. Representations of ram bearers have survived in all forms and shapes. They include marble and bronze statues and statuettes, at least some 200 sarcophagi, wall paintings, pottery lamps, and even objects made of glass. In classical sources, the ram bearer is regarded as a personification of philanthropy. At the same time, such ram bearers also symbolized the timeless happiness of life in the countryside.

Fig. 30. Statue of *kriophoros* or ram bearer. This was a popular type that served to illustrate the attractiveness of rural life.

In the third century A.D. Christians began to adopt the figure of the ram bearer. Christians were interested in this figure for different reasons, namely because it could easily be interpreted as a reference to "the Good Shepherd," that is, a reference to Jesus, "the good shepherd who lies down his life for the sheep," the shepherd who had come "to also lead sheep not belonging to the fold" (John 10).

How popular this theme became, in Christian circles, is evident from study of the large collection of sarcophagi preserved in the Museo Pio Cristiano, which is part of the Vatican museums. On these sarcophagi, the ram bearer appears again and again, and often in a central position. A good example is provided by a sarcophagus that carries the inventory number 191A. On the front of this richly decorated sarcophagus, the ram bearer has been carved no less than three times. To the side of these ram bearers, all of whom carry a curved rod (a typical piece of equipment that characterizes them as shepherds), putti are engaged as part of a vintage scene. On the side of this sarcophagus, personifications of the seasons (spring, summer, autumn, and winter) have been added. The addition of such scenes indicates that these shepherds operate in a world in which idyllic and bucolic or rustic elements set the tone.

The image of the ram bearer appears frequently in the early Christian catacombs of Rome, too, and especially in the oldest parts of those catacombs. This holds true for the Callisto, the Priscilla, and the Domitilla catacombs (in the latter catacomb, there even exists a burial chamber that is known as "Cubiculum of the Good Shepherd"). Every time the ram bearers appears in the catacombs, it is customary to also encounter bucolic and idyllic motifs such as birds, flowers, festoons, and especially peacocks. The presence of such motifs indicates whence the iconography of these figures derives, namely from the world of classical Roman artistic production (fig. 31).

Because of the iconographic neutrality of these motifs, it is frequently rather difficult in individual cases to determine whether a ram bearer should be seen as evidence for Christianity rather than as yet another example of a theme that enjoyed enormous popularity throughout pagan antiquity. In many, although not in all, cases, it is the archaeological context that helps us to settle such questions. Thus, if one finds a wall painting or a sarcophagus with a ram bearer somewhere deep in an early Christian catacomb, one can be relatively

Fig. 31. Wall painting from the Callisto catacomb with an illustration of the *kriophoros*-Good Shepherd.

sure that one is dealing with a work of art commissioned by Christian patrons, by people who saw in this type a reference to the good shepherd and possibly also to the parable of the lost sheep (Luke 15:4-7). Incidentally, the problem of when to identify a ram bearer as "Good Shepherd" is a good illustration of how early Christian art was born within the matrix of non-Christian artistic production.

The use, or better, the adaptation of existing iconographic types such as the fish or the ram bearer constitutes the first step in a process that would soon, in the course of the third century, lead to a process during which existing types where *transformed* so as to conform better to early Christian theological and social needs. As Rome's early Christian community increased in size and became increasingly self-confident, it felt the need to express this newly won self-confidence with artistic means in a more pronounced way than had been the case hitherto. This was a time that new iconographic types and themes were borrowed from the already existing pagan iconographic repertoire for the specific purpose of transforming them into iconographic themes that were specifically Christian.

We have already seen that during the second and third centuries A.D., bucolic and idyllic themes were extremely popular in pagan funerary art. Next to such themes, maritime themes enjoyed great popularity. Given the popularity of such themes, it is not really surprising that one should encounter, in pagan funerary art, representations of figures whose life was in some way associated with the bucolic or the maritime. The ram bearer is one such figure. But not only generic figures occur, also persons known from classical mythology. One of the more popular mythological figures was Endymion. He was a beautiful youth who had been submersed in an everlasting sleep by the moon goddess Selene. Other figures that enjoyed popularity include the Greek singer Orpheus, whose music was said to have had an enchanting effect on both people and animals. And then there also was Deucalion, another Greek, who, together with his wife, had managed to survive in a boat when the earth had been hit by an enormous flood ordained by the Greek god Zeus.

As is evident from wall paintings that have been preserved in the early Christian catacombs of Rome, Christians began to copy these types and transform them into figures that had a special meaning for Christians, and for Christians only. Thus the sleeping youth Endymion was adopted, but he was also transformed during this process of adoption, namely into the biblical figure of Jonah, the biblical prophet who was sent to persuade the inhabitants of Nineveh into giving up their all too lax way of life (fig. 32). At first sight, hardly any transformation seems to have taken place in those paintings in the catacombs that represent Jonah: we still see a young man, naked, with the same features and stance as his pagan counterpart Endymion (his reclining posture, with his arm over his head is typically classical; in this way Roman artists represented a person that was sound asleep).

When we look somewhat more carefully, however, we can begin to see that some changes in this classical iconographic type have taken place. Thus, several additions can be

Fig. 32. Jonah-cycle from the Callisto catacomb. The cycle includes: Jonah being thrown overboard, Jonah disgorged by a *ketos*, and Jonah resting. Formally, Jonah looks identical with Endymion.

discerned that are absent in earlier pagan depictions, but that turn out to belong to the standard repertoire of motifs that accompany this resting youth when he appears in early Christian iconographic contexts. One such addition, for example, is a pergola. The presence of such a pergola is not accidental: it is an allusion to the "climbing gourd" mentioned in the biblical book that describes the story of Jonah (4:6-8). Good examples of such pergolas can also be found on the sarcophagi of the Museo Pio Cristiano.

In addition to these representations that show a reclining youth, other scenes also begin to appear. It is not unusual to see in the art of the catacombs representations of a ship and of someone who is cast overboard. Yet another scene, namely that of a sea monster that spits out a man, also occurs frequently. All of these representations are classical insofar as their formal appearance is concerned. Thus the sea monster mentioned previously takes on the form of a dragon that belongs to a type that was very popular in Roman art during the first few centuries of the Common Era. Still, the classical appearance of these representations cannot mislead us. We are no longer looking at some story derived from classical mythology. What we have here is a more or less coherent sequence of scenes that illustrate various stages in the story of Jonah (Jonah cast into the sea; Jonah disgorged by the monster; Jonah resting).

It is interesting to note that additions such as the ones we have just described were not limited to the story of Jonah. Also in case of the other mythological figures mentioned previously, additions were carried out by Christians so as to transform these classical heroes into biblical personalities. Thus, the addition of a bird in case of representations of Deucalion suggests that the people ordering such paintings no longer thought of Deucalion, but had Noah and the story of the Flood in mind. Even though the pagan roots of such representations are unmistakable, the Christian interpretations given to them are no less apparent, at least for those familiar with the biblical text.

That this process of transformation was not only limited to the wall paintings in the catacomb, but occurred elsewhere as well, becomes evident when we turn to the large collection of sarcophagi preserved in the Museo Pio Cristiano. One of the sarcophagi there (inventory number 119) contains a full rendering of the story of Jonah, a rendering of this story in three episodes: Jonah cast into the sea; Jonah disgorged by the monster; Jonah resting (fig. 33). These three episodes occur in a setting that contains a variety of idyllic and maritime motifs, such as a fishing scene on the lower right side of the sarcophagus, and a shepherd scene on the sarcophagus' upper right. Noah and his ark have also been represented (they are fairly small and appear on top of the sea monster). They take on the form of a little man in a box, complete with little bird (see Genesis 8:6-13). Further biblical themes also appear on this sarcophagus – themes we have not yet encountered. They include Moses drawing water from the rock (Exodus 17:6) as well as the raising of Lazarus from the dead (John 11).

Fig. 33. Sarcophagus with Jonah-cycle, bucolic and idyllic themes, and the raising of Lazarus.

As is evident from the size in which the various themes have been rendered, the story of Jonah is still the single most prominent item on this sarcophagus. At the same time, however, other biblical stories begin to appear. As we will see in greater detail later on, it was such other stories that would began to replace, in the later third century, the representations that were less outspokenly Christian such as those of the good shepherd and even that of Jonah.

These examples show that the process of transformation we have been studying concerns primarily the content or iconography of the scenes represented. Technically and stylistically no major changes can be discerned. In fact, on that level the continuity between pagan and early Christian art is as strong as a continuity can be.

In light of this observation, it should not surprise us that recent research has shown that Christians employed exactly the same workshops as did their non-Christian contemporaries. Such workshops simply catered to a variety of customers including Christian ones. These workshops mass-produced sarcophagi and wall paintings with bucolic and idyllic themes. Evidently Christians found such themes alluring, all the more so because they were often iconographically neutral (from a religious point of view) and also, of course, because such themes could easily be transformed into representations of stories that were meaningful to them as Christians.

As experimenting with existing iconographic types and with the transformation of these types into representations that were specifically Christian was becoming increasingly common, in the later third century Christians started to feel more confident and began to develop – on a larger scale and in a more systematic fashion than ever before – a new and typically Christian iconographic repertoire. To judge on the basis of the wall paintings that have survived in the catacombs, it seems that within this new and typically Christian iconographic repertoire, scenes derived from the Old Testament were initially at least three times as popular as those derived from the New Testament. In addition to depictions of the story of Jonah – a theme that in the late third century continues to outrank all other biblical scenes in popularity, especially in the Callisto and Domitilla catacombs – we now begin to encounter more or less regularly depictions of the sacrifice of Isaac (Genesis 22); of the three Hebrews in the fiery furnace (Daniel 3; occurs several times in the Domitilla and Priscilla catacombs); and of Daniel in the lions' den (Daniel 6; occurs in the Domitilla and Callisto catacombs). Throughout the third century, scenes taken from the New Testament remain an exception that confirms the rule. The only two New Testament scenes that occur with some regularity, are the baptism of Christ in the river Jordan (Matthew 3:13-17) and the resurrection of Lazarus (John 11; this occurs notably in wall paintings in the Domitilla and Callisto catacombs).

Insofar as their composition is concerned, the representations of Old and New Testament scenes have much in common. Almost always one encounters isolated episodes instead of narrative cycles. Such episodes are normally painted on a neutral or white surface. Indications of a landscape or of an urban setting in which such biblical stories are known to have taken place, are usually absent. The "simplification" by which biblical stories are reduced to single, isolated episodes has led some scholars to believe that early Christian art drew its principal inspiration from decorated rings such as those described by Clement (such rings offer limited space), but further research is necessary to determine the usefulness of such a hypothesis.

Good examples of this newly-emerging, typically Christian iconographic repertoire can be found in the so-called Sacrament Chapels in the Callisto catacomb. In reality, these chapels are a series of burial rooms that date to the first half of the third century and that have been decorated with scenes taken from the Old as well as the New Testament. Among the scenes represented we encounter: the story of Jonah, the story of Noah, the sacrifice of Isaac, Moses drawing water from the rock, the baptism of Christ, the healing of the lame, the raising of Lazarus from the dead, and Christ and the woman of Samaria at the well.

Other good examples of the concurrent appearance of Old and New Testament scenes have been preserved in the Capella Greca in the Priscilla catacomb (late third century). There wall paintings can be found that depict the raising of Lazarus from the dead, Daniel in the lions' den, the sacrifice of Isaac, the three Hebrews in the fiery furnace, Susanna and the elders, Noah, Moses drawing water from the rock, the baptism of Christ, the healing of the lame and the adoration of the Magi.

A closer look at all these third century paintings reveals that they have several things in common. It has already been observed that during this period, stories taken from the Old Testament were much more popular than those taken from the New Testament (fig 34). To this can be added that with regard to the stories that were actually chosen for representation, Christians seem to have preferred the depiction of a limited selection of stories only.

The just-mentioned wall paintings in the Callisto and Priscilla catacombs show that while a limited selection of biblical stories appear again and again on the walls of these subterranean cemeteries, representations of other biblical stories that would have been equally fitting in this context appear

Fig. 34. Wall painting of
Moses striking the rock
(Exodus 17:5-6).

not even once. During this period, the repertoire of themes
selected remains extremely limited.

With regard to the New Testament scenes, it can be
observed that in all these paintings, Christ is rendered as a
young man. In these renditions, especially where the formal
and stylistic characteristics of these depictions are concerned,
one can still see how such depictions are indebted to classical
Roman art. Thus such depictions provide us with yet another
example of how early Christian art drew much of its initial
inspiration from Roman art. It is not until the fourth century
that Christ is rendered in a more majestic fashion, and as an
older, bearded man (note that in this later period, depictions
of Christ as a young man do not disappear altogether). During this same period, depictions of the suffering of Christ also
begin to appear. In the third century, such representations are
still absent (there is only one exception, namely wall paintings
in the Prestestato catacomb).

The popularity of Old Testament scenes in early Christian
art throughout the third century is especially remarkable

when one realizes that the essence of Christianity is not to be found in the Old Testament but rather in the New. It is only in the New Testament that we find a long expose of the life and sufferings of Christ, and of the meaning that is to be attributed to his coming to this world. If this is so, why then would Rome's early Christian community have preferred the rendition of Old Testament scenes over New Testament ones?

Scholars have long tried to find an explanation for this phenomenon. Let us pause to briefly investigate their theories. As we will now see, an investigation of such theories is interesting because it will help us to place the emergence of early Christian art into a larger artistic as well as social context.

## Possible Explanations

One of the more popular theories scholars have formulated to explain why early Christian art did not emerge until fairly late in the history of Rome's early Christian community focuses on evidence that can be derived from early Christian writings dating to the second and third centuries A.D. The authors of such writings, who are called apologists, fulminate at length against the pagan usage of decorating temples and homes with representations of gods and mythological figures. Such fulminations were based on a strict interpretation of a biblical text in Exodus 20:4-5, "You must not make a carved image for yourself, nor the likeness of anything in the heavens above, or on the earth below, or in the waters under the earth. You must not bow down to them in worship, for I the Lord your God, am a jealous God etc."

Taking into account such ideas, scholars believed that the absence of early Christian art during the first two centuries could be explained by saying that fear for idolatry caused a general aversion to art and artistic production that went beyond early Christian literary circles. Pointing out that some (although certainly not all) later church fathers also disapproved of representing Christ in an artistic fashion, scholars have hypothesized furthermore that when early Christian art finally started to emerge in the course of the third century, such an emergence is likely to have been due to the "subversive" initiatives of lay people, that is, of Christians who were not part of the ecclesiastical establishment and who were not at home in the intricacies of early Christian scriptural exegesis and theology.

Upon closer consideration, the above explanation is not entirely satisfactory. Recent research of these early Christian apologetic writers has shown that their critique of pagan practices was mainly fueled by the desire to create a contrast that could serve help highlight the more congenial aspects of their own (Christian) religion. According to this line of reasoning, the purpose of the apologists' critique was primarily rhetorical: by underlining that current pagan practices were silly, early Christian writers hoped to curry favor for their own religion – a religion that was new, not yet established, and, from a pagan perspective, peculiar in many ways. Put differently, this new scholarly approach to the writings of the apologists maintains that early Christian writers did not dislike art per se; they only disliked the abuses that were caused, in certain pagan circles, by the use of art (they especially disliked idolatry). Scholars who propagate this line of reasoning also maintain that the idea that early Christian art originated in certain Christian circles that knew little about Christian theology or that cared little about it is to be rejected, primarily for lack of ancient evidence that could support such a view. Because such explanations are no longer considered satisfactory, scholars have begun to prefer explanations that are more straightforward in that they also take into account the "practical" aspects of the process that led to the emergence of early Christian art.

In the preceding pages we have seen that early Christian art emerged gradually, as part of artistic trends that are not exclusively Christian, but that can be discerned in other artistic contexts as well. Upon closer consideration, it is not really surprising for these developments to have taken place in this fashion. After all, most members of Rome's early Christian community were converts who had a pagan background. Such people simply continued, once they had been converted, to use those objects they had always used. In many cases, conversion simply did not mean that all contacts with contemporary society were discontinued. In fact, often the opposite seems to have been the case.

There was one factor in particular that determined why people used, and continued to use, certain objects and artifacts. Starting in the first century A.D., many objects and artifacts were produced in Rome in large workshops. Labor in such workshops was divided so as to permit the production of large amounts of artifacts and objects according to standardized lines of production. Such standardization of the production process resulted in a sizable increase of objects and artifacts produced. It was with these mass-produced objects and artifacts that workshops flooded the market. Dominating the art market in this fashion, it were these workshops that set the standard for both the style and iconography of objects and artifacts that were available to the public at large.

Good examples of how to visualize this process can be found by looking at the evidence provided by Roman sarcophagi produced during this period. Such sarcophagi divide into several groups that can be distinguished on the basis of their iconography. The existence of just a few of such standard groups shows that the influence individual customers could exert on a design was in most cases fairly limited: workshops just produced one sarcophagus after the next, all with similar iconography, and according to standard production procedures. A careful investigation of the traces left by the tools of the stonecutters indicates, interestingly, that different stonecutters were responsible for different stages in the production of a sarcophagus. The whole process of production consisted of a series of carefully arranged stages. At each stage, there were different workers who were responsible for a limited number of tasks only.

Similar developments can also be discerned where the history of late antique Roman wall painting is concerned. Our evidence suggests that here too, during certain periods, certain standardized styles and iconographies became so popular that they began to replace all other pictorial styles available at the time. The red-green linear style that we encounter in the late second and early third century, everywhere in Roman houses as well as in many cubiculums in the catacombs (fig. 35), is a good example of such a style that was the trademark of workshops that effectively handled one large commission after the other (this pictorial style occurs frequently in the Domitilla, Sebastiano and Callisto catacombs).

Once we take into account the developments that have been sketched here, it becomes possible to better understand how early Christian art originated. When Christianity appeared on the scene, Christian art did not exist, but still had to be invented. What did exist at this time were Roman workshops that dominated the art market. In such a situation it was only natural for Christians, many of whom were converts from paganism, to make use of the artistic objects and artifacts that were commonly available. As time went on, Christians felt the need to express their identity through art.

Fig. 35. Example of the
red-green linear style.
Vigna Randanini
catacomb.

In the preceding pages we have seen that they did so by adapting current iconographic schemata and themes, in due course transforming these into an artistic language that, from an iconographic point of view, was typically Christian. This process of transformation was a gradual one. Especially in the beginning Christians continued to make use of mentioned workshops. They just asked these artists to make little changes here and there. Such artists responded by making use of the classical repertoire they were used to. Thus, when Christian customers wanted a representation of Jonah, the artist used Endymion for this purpose, turning him into Jonah by adding a pergola. Despite its classical appearance, Christians could understand such a pergola as a reference to the climbing gourd of the biblical story. The emergence of early Christian art can, in short, best be seen as a evolutionary process during which Christians developed – slowly but certainly and starting with an artistic basis that was definitely non-Christian – iconographic preferences that were more and more distinctly Christian as time went by.

It is not so easy, on the other hand, to explain the early Christian, third century preference for scenes taken from the Old Testament, or to determine why Christian preferred certain New Testament scenes to others. Looking somewhat more carefully at the biblical scenes that appear in the oldest parts of the catacombs, it is nonetheless possible to discern a common theme behind these scenes, independent of whether they were taken from the Old or the New Testament. All the representations we have discussed in previous pages illustrate the power of God as well as his willingness to save those who truly believe in him. The story of Jonah illustrates this concept just as well as does the story of the raising of Lazarus from the dead. Stories such as the sacrifice of Isaac, the three Hebrews in the fiery furnace, or Daniel in the lions' den can likewise all be taken as illustrations of God's saving power. That the idea of an omnipotent God must have appealed to the people who were buried in the catacombs goes without saying (fig. 36).

It is conceivable that still other factors played a role here too – factors that can help to explain the early Christian preference for the Old Testament. In roughly the same period that scenes taken from the Old Testament appear on the walls of the catacombs, Christian theologians began to develop the concept of *verus Israel*. *Verus Israel* is Latin for "the true Israel." This concept was developed by early Christian theologians in an attempt to turn Christianity into a religion that was acceptable to non-Christians, if not on a religious, at least on a social and political level.

In the ancient world, respectability depended on age: while in Roman eyes religions with a long history were respectable, religions which could not lay claim to such ancient traditions were not. Being a relatively new religion

Fig. 36. Shadrach, Meshach, and Abednego in the fiery furnace (Daniel 3). Jordanorum catacomb. Drawing from the time of the Counterreformation.

(one that had come into existence only in the first century A.D.), Christianity lacked those credentials necessary in order to be taken seriously by ancient society at large. As Christianity hoped to acquire as many converts as possible, Christian writers were bothered by the lack of respect that Christianity suffered in non-Christian circles. They began looking for an old tradition to which Christianity could lay claim. They found that tradition in the Hebrew Bible. In that Bible they found many useful traditions – traditions that, moreover, could be interpreted in such a way as to suggest that the coming of Christian Messiah (namely, Jesus), had been predicted in these ancient and honorable books. Instead of calling these books the Hebrew Bible, early Christian writers preferred calling them the *Old* Testament, thus suggesting that the Hebrew Bible was nothing but a companion volume to their own *New* Testament. Even though the Hebrew Bible/Old Testament really belonged to the Jews, such writers claimed furthermore that the Jews had lost the rights accorded to them by God because they had refused to convert to Christianity. As they were inspecting the Old Testament and appropriating it for their own purposes, early Christian writers saw no problem in presenting themselves as the real heirs to that old tradition. They thus argued that they represented the true Israel.

Such a state of affairs is quite interesting and may help to explain why the Old Testament was held in such high esteem in early Christian circles. On the one hand, it was the Old Testament that gave Christianity its *raison d'être* – at least partially. On the other hand, the Old Testament, a book rich in stories and adventures, provided Christians not merely with a rich repertoire of scenes that could be illustrated, but also with accounts that could be interpreted as references to the life and sufferings of Christ. It was this "typological" approach according to which such Old Testament stories were seen as prefigurations or prototypes of the events told in the New Testament that was to have a lasting effect on the development of early Christian art in the fourth century, as we will now see.

## The New Testament Phase

In the fourth century, major changes affected the early Christian community, not only in Rome, but in other parts of the Empire as well. Starting with the promulgation of the Edict of Milan in A.D. 313, Christians were now accorded the same rights as the adherents of other religions in the Empire. As a result of this Edict, Christianity could now develop more freely than ever before. In the course of the fourth century, ever larger groups of people converted to Christianity. This development reached its peak in A.D. 391 when Christianity was declared the state religion.

As Christianity developed as a religious movement, the importance of which no one could deny any longer, early Christian art began to undergo a thorough transformation. Early Christian wall paintings and sarcophagi dating to this period indicate that from the fourth century onwards early Christian art was no longer the result of forces on which Christians could exert their influence only to a limited degree, as had been the case previously when Christians had employed types and schemata that had been developed in Roman, non-Christian workshops. Instead now works of art were produced that were specifically Christian in their iconography (fig. 37). Motifs such as the ram bearer disappear, to be replaced by motifs that no longer have their roots entirely in the world of pagan artistic production. It is the New Testament that now begins to form the most important source of inspiration for artists and patrons alike.

To sketch the developments that characterize this period in the history of early Christian art, it is best to turn, once again, to the archaeological materials that have been preserved in the early Christian catacombs of Rome, and to early Christian sarcophagi in particular.[1] The easiest way to familiarize oneself with these sarcophagi is by visiting the impressive collection

Fig. 37. Christ enthroned (*Maiestas Domini*). Mosaic on the back wall of an arcosolium in the Domitilla catacomb. Such mosaic decorations are rare in the catacombs.

---

[1] It is likely that during this same period, early Christian art "above ground" underwent dramatic changes too. We know, for example, that this was a time during which the first truly monumental early Christian churches were constructed. Yet, the evidence bearing on these early Christian remains is limited. Therefore, only finds in the catacombs provide us with the evidence that permits us to determine how early Christian art developed during this period.

of early Christian sarcophagi preserved in the Museo Pio Cristiano (part of the Vatican museums). Even a brief glance at the sarcophagi that have been exhibited here suffices to show what kind of changes have taken place in the field of early Christian artistic production. Most notably, Old Testament scenes have begun to lose their place of prominence. In their place come New Testament scenes. They now outnumber Old Testament in the same way they were outnumbered by Old Testament ones in the previous century.

No less visible is the fact that from this time onwards many more scenes have been selected from the New Testament. Consequently, the iconographic variety has increased considerably. Of all New Testament figures that appear on these sculpted containers, Jesus is given a place of central importance. Such importance is stressed visually in a number of different ways: by placing Christ in the center of a sarcophagus relief, by making him larger than the other figures around him, and by thematically arranging the scenes selected around the events that determined the course of His life. The frequent use of sarcophagi with little niches flanked by columns permitted artists to render various events next to one another. Of all events that are normally included, those events that illustrate Christ's sufferings are by far the most popular.

It has already been observed that despite the importance of New Testament scenes, Old Testament scenes do not disappear entirely from the early Christian iconographic repertoire during the fourth century. The reason for this continued popularity of Old Testament scenes has to be sought in the importance attributed to the idea that there existed a typological relationship between both Testaments. According to this idea, many events in the Old Testament could be read or interpreted as prefigurations of symbolic announcements of events described in the New Testament. Thus, the story of Job was viewed as prefiguring the sufferings of Christ, just as the sacrifice of Isaac was interpreted as a prototype of the Crucifixion of Christ. The role played by this idea in fourth Christian theology also helps to explain why, during this period, certain Old Testament scenes were so popular in the art of the catacombs and others were not.

One of the earliest Christian sarcophagi and one that can serve to illustrate these developments is one that served as final resting place for a certain Junius Bassus. Junius Bassus was a high Roman official who had been baptized just before he died on the 25th of August of the year A.D. 359 (fig. 38). He was buried in a richly decorated sarcophagus – a real masterpiece that is on display in the Museo Pio Cristiano. The main decoration of this piece, which has been decorated

Fig. 38. Front side of the sarcophagus of Junius Bassus who died on August 25, 359 AD. In the center, a youthful Christ has been rendered.
The other niches contain scenes from Christ's life on earth, as well as of several Old Testament scenes that can be interpreted as prefiguring the life and sufferings of Christ (typology).

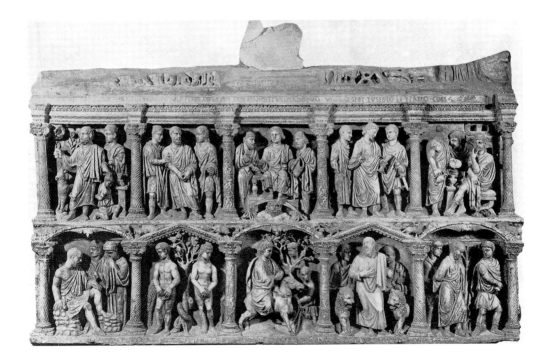

on three sides, can be found on the front side of the sarcophagus. It consists of a series of niches with sculpted figures. The niches have been arranged in two horizontal rows. The central niche contains a representation of a young Christ with the apostles Peter and Paul on his side. Directly below him, a bust of a man can be seen. He is to be regarded as personification of the skies (*Caelus*). To the left and right of this central niche, further niches can be found with events from Jesus' life, but also with scenes taken from the Old Testament. All these Old Testament scenes have to be understood typologically: they were selected because they prefigure the life and suffering of Christ. The scenes represented include, from left to right: the sacrifice of Isaac, the arrest of Peter, Christ on a throne, the arrest of Christ, and Pilate washing his hands (upper register); Job sitting on a dung-hill, the Temptation of Adam and Eve, Jesus entering Jerusalem, Daniel in the lions' den, and the arrest of Paul. On both sides of the sarcophagus traditional idyllic motifs have been carved, complete with putti and vintage scenes.

Sarcophagi like that of Junius Bassus provide us with interesting evidence to show that from this period onwards, changes begin to manifest themselves with regard to the way Christ is represented. Even though Christ is still represented as a young man on some of these sarcophagi, his presence becomes much more important and central than had been the case hitherto. This is particularly evident on a sarcophagus in the Museo Pio Cristiano that carries the inventory number 138. On this sarcophagus Christ is depicted in the very center of this stone container. Three men who carry scrolls surround him. Their identity remains unknown. They are probably apostles. This sarcophagus, which dates to the second half of the fourth century, helps to document the shift from an early Christian art that is generally late antique to one that is specifically Christian. The emphasis on the figure of Christ (Christology) is the single most important characteristic of this specifically Christian art.

The emphasis on the figure of Christ gave rise, in the course of the fourth century, to still another type of sarcophagus: the passion sarcophagus. Sarcophagi belonging to this group derive their name from the iconography that appears on them. Such sarcophagi illustrate various aspects of Christ's sufferings. That these sufferings appear on early Christian sarcophagi at all is interesting. Earlier, in the third century, Christians had specifically refrained from depictions of Christ's crucifixion, because such crucifixions were considered as something shameful. In Roman law, crucifixion was reserved for criminals of the worst kind. The fact that such depictions of crucifixion scenes begin to appear in early Christian art in the course of the fourth century can be seen as a good indication for the self-confidence that permeated early Christian circles during this period. One event in particular contributed to the popularity of this kind of depictions in the fourth century. In A.D. 312, just before a determinative battle at the Milvian bridge (near Rome) during which he won a resounding victory over one of his pagan opponents, Constantine had witnessed the sign of a cross in the skies and had heard the words "in this sign you will conquer." Constantine had his soldiers paint the cross on their shields. They won the battle. From that moment onwards, the cross was no longer a symbol of shame. It became a sign of victory, the single most popular symbol Christian artists ever produced.

It hardly needs to be stressed that in the centuries that followed, the cross came to be Christianity's symbol *par excellence*. It is interesting to stress that the beginnings of this development can be dated to precisely the fourth century.

That the cross rapidly became a really popular symbol is evident when we inspect, once again, the sarcophagus collection of the Museo Pio Cristiano. On some sarcophagi preserved there (such as the one with inventory number 171) the central niche is no longer occupied by Christ, but by a rendition of the cross (note that in the case of this sarcophagus, the cross has also been rendered a christogram, or symbol representing, in abbreviated fashion, the name of Christ.) The sarcophagus in question, incidentally, belongs to the type of passion sarcophagus mentioned previously. From left to right we see representations of Simon of Cyrene carrying the cross, a soldier who puts a laurel wreath (a sign of victory) instead of a crown of thorns on Jesus' head, the cross, Christ with a soldier, and Pilate washing his hands.

Even though, therefore, early Christian art can be said to have come of age in the course of the fourth century, such a development did not automatically mean that the "pagan" elements that had played such an important role in early Christian art during the third century disappeared altogether. The best example of how pagan pictorial traditions survived well into the fourth century can be found in a small catacomb on the Via Latina (not normally open to the public). This catacomb is interesting, not only because pagans and Christians were buried in it side by side. The catacomb is interesting also because of the magnificent paintings that survive in it. Next to scenes taken from the Old and New Testaments, we encounter a rich selection of mythological stories on the wall of this incredibly beautiful monument. The presence of such mythological themes suggests that even though paganism may have been on the wane in the later fourth century, the artistic traditions it had produced were still very much alive.

With these developments the history of early Christian art insofar as it can be reconstructed on the basis of the evidence from the catacombs comes to a close (fig. 39). Starting in the fifth century, the catacombs were no longer used for burial on any systematic scale. Even though walls in the catacombs continued to be decorated with wall paintings, such efforts are the exception that confirms the rule. In the catacombs, artistic production now comes to an almost complete halt. The few paintings that were still produced during this time, especially to embellish the graves of the martyrs, pale in comparison to the number of paintings that were produced in the catacombs during the first few centuries. That such early medieval paintings are isolated cases that do not permit us to reconstruct the development of Christian art during this time as a whole is obvious enough.

Fig. 39. Raising of Lazarus. Wall painting from the Domitilla catacomb. Lazarus who looks like a mummy, is standing in a mausoleum. A youthful Christ calls him back from the dead.

Last but not least, a few words should be said about the possible influence of ancient Jewish art on early Christian art. Following a series of spectacular discoveries of Jewish archaeological remains in Israel and elsewhere in the Mediterranean, scholars have begun to hypothesize about the possible influence of Jewish on early Christian art. The rationale for such endeavors is simple. If there once existed Jewish art, as can no longer be denied, and taking into account that Judaism preceded Christianity as a religion, then the idea that Jews may have influenced Christians in the arts as well becomes a real possibility.

Although much research remains to be done in this area, it is certain that the influence of Jewish on early Christian art must have been fairly limited, at least insofar as the Roman evidence is concerned. The hypothesis that there once existed illustrated Jewish Bibles that served as a source of inspiration for Christians cannot be proven. Not only does it happen to be the case that no such Bible has survived. We do not even know whether they ever existed at all. Another important argument that seems to make the idea of large-scale Jewish influence unlikely is the fact that early Christian art developed gradually out of Roman art, as has become evident in the course of this chapter. The evidence provided by the Jewish catacombs of Rome (for more details, Appendix I) finally also seems to indicate that we should rule out the possibility of direct Jewish influence. In the wall paintings that have survived in the Jewish catacombs, scenes taken from the Old Testament or Hebrew Bible are absent altogether. Instead, what appears are symbols that are definitely Jewish and that show no connection with the iconography we encounter in the Christian catacombs. Recent research has shown that in Rome Jewish art developed along the same lines as early Christian art: Jews employed Roman workshops that produced works of art Jews found suitable because they permitted, within a typically Roman iconographic and stylistic framework, the insertion of symbols that were typically and unmistakably Jewish. This is not to deny the influence of Judaism on Christianity. Yet, it should be stressed that at least where Rome is concerned, this influence manifested itself in areas other than artistic.

On the basis of this exposé, it may have become clear that the material evidence preserved in the early Christian catacombs of Rome deserves the full attention of anyone interested in the history of Christianity. It is in these catacombs that we find the earliest examples of iconographic patterns and themes that would shape the history of European art for almost two millennia. Without these remains, it would be impossible to know how this tradition originated, and what motivated the people responsible for its invention.

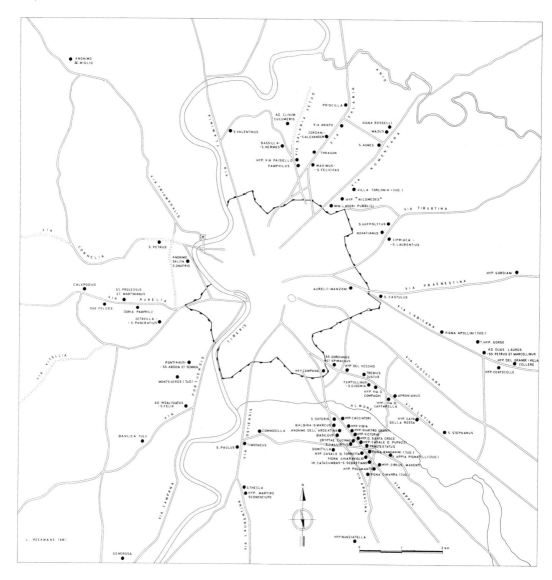

Fig. 40. Plan of Rome, with an indication of the consular roads and of the city's most important catacombs.

# CHAPTER 4

# Guide to the Catacombs
# Open to the General Public

## Introduction

Some sixty catacombs have been discovered in and around Rome (fig. 40). Of these sixty catacombs, only a few are open to the general public, mostly the larger ones. By visiting one or more of these catacombs, it is possible to gain a better understanding of some of the issues that have been raised in the previous chapters of this book. While a visit to the Priscilla, Domitilla, Sebastiano, or Callisto catacombs is especially worthwhile, a visit to the Agnese catacomb is perhaps somewhat less interesting for non-specialists. Inasmuch as the works of art preserved in Rome's subsoil differ from one catacomb to the next, visitors who are really interested in the art and archaeology of the catacombs should consider descending into more than just one catacomb. Visitors to Rome are also advised to visit the so-called Vatican necropolis. In this necropolis, which is located under St. Peter's, visitors can stroll around in a typical second-century Roman necropolis. In addition, visitors to this cemetery can also gain a better understanding of the complex architectural context in which the grave of the apostle Peter was recovered.

With the exception of the Vatican necropolis (for details, see below), tourists can visit the catacombs by joining tours that depart regularly from the catacomb's entrance (reservations are not necessary). Tour guides speak several languages, including English. On average, such a tour in the catacombs lasts thirty to forty-five minutes.

Visitors to the catacombs should be aware that the atmosphere in these subterranean places is fairly humid and that temperatures are more or less constant. This means that whereas in the summer it is fairly cool and humid in the catacombs, in the winter it is fairly warm and humid there. Because of the humidity and because the level of oxygen can at times be slightly lower than above ground, people who suffer from respiratory diseases or claustrophobia should be careful about entering the catacombs. Visitors do not need to bring their own flashlights. In those parts of the catacombs that are accessible to the general public, electric lights have been installed.

People who are interested in visiting catacombs that are not normally open to the public should apply in writing to the Pontificia Commissione di Archeologia Sacra, Via Napoleone III, 1, 00185, Rome, tel. 06-446 5610; fax 06-446 7625. The Jewish catacombs of Rome fall under the jurisdiction of the Archaeological Superintendency. They can be visited only on rare occasions. Groups who would like to celebrate mass in the catacombs are advised to contact the officials responsible for the catacomb in question in advance (for telephone numbers, see below).

In the following pages, practical information is given concerning the catacombs that are open to the public. Also included is a short discussion of the finds visitors can expect to see, with special emphasis on the issues that have been discussed in previous chapters. With regard to the opening hours mentioned here, it is important to stress that these may be subject to (sudden) change. The logic for such sudden changes escapes even experienced researchers.

### The Catacombs on the Internet (Fall 1999)

A useful multi-language internet site containing information concerning the catacombs can be found at http://www. catacombe.roma.it. The site contains a series of photos in color as well as a number of pages with information on the catacombs. Special emphasis is placed on the Callisto catacomb complex. Although the site is arranged well, it should be observed that the information it contains does not always reflect the latest scholarly thinking in matters relating to catacomb archaeology. Containing the text of an address by Pope John Paul II concerning the importance of the catacombs as well as the text of several prayers for the Jubilee indulgence, the site is especially useful for pilgrims. The site finally also contains two quizzes that can be used to test one's knowledge regarding the catacombs.

The official multi-language site for the Jubilee can be found at http://www.jubil2000.org. This site contains information concerning the catacombs, albeit in a more concise manner that the internet site mentioned previously. Especially interesting are a series of short movie fragments (http://www.jubil2000.org/catacombe/catacombe.it.html).

## CATACOMB OF CALLISTO

Address: Via Appia Antica 110. Opening hours 8:30-12:00 a.m. and 2:30-5:30 p.m. Closed on Wednesdays and in February. Tel. 06-5136725. Fax 06-51301567.

Transportation: bus 218 (leaves at the Piazza S. Giovanni in Laterano = Metro Linea A, stop San Giovanni). Get out at the church "Domine Quo Vadis?" Then, on foot to the catacomb. Enter the gate located between the Via Appia Antica and the

Via Ardeatina, and follow the asphalted road that leads to the catacomb (approx. 10 minutes; here one can enjoy a beautiful view of the Aurelian city wall and of the Porta San Sebastiano). The catacomb can also be reached by car (enter by the same gate). A parking lot is located near the catacomb.

Tour includes: the oldest region in the catacomb, including the "crypt of the popes" (see Chapters 1 and 2), the crypt of Santa Caecilia, the Sacrament chapels (Chapter 3) as well as the cubiculum of pope Eusebius.

Description: The Callisto catacomb is Rome's early Christian catacomb par excellence. The first phase in the building history of this catacomb dates to the early third century. At that time a series of galleries was excavated under the supervision of the deacon Calixtus (hence the name of the catacomb). Serving to bury the poorer members of Rome's early Christian community, these galleries constitute the first real early Christian communal underground cemetery (see also Chapter 2).

The Callisto catacomb is famous for other reasons too, however. It was here, in the "crypt of the popes," that many third century popes found their final resting place. In Chapter 1 we have already discussed how the nineteenth-century rediscovery of this crypt helped to revitalize public interest in catacomb archaeology.

It was in the Callisto catacomb, to be precise in A.D. 258, that pope Sixtus II was killed during a persecution of Christians. The story of his assassination later gave rise to the erroneous assumption according to which the early Christian catacombs of Rome primarily served as places where Christians hid from persecutions (see Chapter 1).

From an archaeological perspective, the Callisto catacomb has much in common with some of the other large early Christian catacombs of Rome, such as the Domitilla and Sebastiano complexes (fig. 41). The Callisto catacomb extends under an area with mausolea on the surface. These mausolea had been enlarged in due course through underground extensions (on these developments, see Chapter 2). These underground extensions formed the nucleus of the later catacomb. Especially from the fourth century onwards, the Callisto catacomb developed into an enormous underground cemetery with galleries on four different levels, totaling a length of 20 kilometers.

The "crypt of the popes" is one of the most interesting and also one of the oldest sections in the Callisto catacomb. It can be reached through a hallway the walls of which have been covered with graffiti left there by pilgrims. These graffiti show how popular a visit to this crypt must have been in late

Fig. 41. Callisto catacomb. Banquet scene (*refrigerium*) with seven participants. The banquet motif is of pagan origin.

antique and early medieval times. The actual "crypt of the popes" consists of four niches designed for sarcophagi and of twelve loculi graves that were used to bury a number of popes whose papacy can be dated to the period from A.D. 235 to 283. That this is so follows from a monumental inscription erected in the fourth century by pope Damasus (this inscription, which was rediscovered by de Rossi, can be still be seen in its original location). Some of the architectural decoration in the crypt of the popes such as the columns and architraves (moulded crossbeam) as well as the marble screens are also due to the intervention of pope Damasus.

Other early nuclei in the Callisto catacomb can be found in the direct vicinity of the "crypt of the popes." Tradition has it that Saint Caecilia, the patron saint of music, was buried in one of the cubicles that are connected to the "crypt of the popes."

In the same general area can also be found a sequence of six cubicles that are known as the Sacraments Chapels. These rooms are interesting because of the painted decoration they contain. Here we encounter excellent examples of the Old Testament phase in early Christian art (see Chapter 3). Stories represented include: the story of Jonah, Noah, the sacrifice of Isaac, Moses drawing water from the rock (Exodus 17:6), the baptism of Christ, the healing of the lame, the raising of Lazarus from the dead, Christ and the woman of Samaria at the well.

The Sacrament Chapels are connected to an area consisting of long underground galleries. Archaeologists refer to this area as Area I. They identify it as the area where the deacon Calixtus created his cemetery for the poor. The area in question consists of a series of long, straight galleries that have all been excavated in such a way as to permit the inhumation of large groups of people and that are connected to one another by means of a series of transverse galleries. The area thus provides us with one of the earliest examples of rational planning, a type of catacomb design that was to become the standard way of catacomb planning in subsequent decades (and especially from the fourth century onwards, when catacombs began to develop into underground cemeteries of enormous proportion).

In another area not far removed from this Area I, we encounter the grave of pope Eusebius (A.D. 310-311). He too was to receive a commemorative inscription by the hand of Damasus (cited in Chapter 2). Other cubicles in this area contain wall paintings with a paradise garden (the idyllic theme), a "Good Shepherd" (the bucolic theme), and several scenes derived from both the Old and New Testaments. It was in this area that de Rossi discovered, in the nineteenth century, an inscription that dates to the early fourth century and that is regarded as the oldest piece of evidence for the use of the term *pope* (namely *papa*, which literally means father).

Continuing our journey we arrive in a part of the catacomb that dates to the fourth century. It is usually referred to as the region of Pope Liberius (A.D. 352-366). This region is interesting because of its wall paintings. These paintings include a depiction of the feeding of the five thousand, the raising of Lazarus from the dead, and of Christ, represented here with beard and nimbus.

The famous "crypt of Lucina" can be found in a still different part of the catacomb, in an underground section located close to the Via Appia Antica. Lucina's crypt is especially interesting because of the wall paintings that survive. They belong to the oldest phase of early Christian art. They include a famous representation of a fish with a basket on top, and renderings of two "Good Shepherds," of praying figures, of Daniel in the lions' den, and of the baptism of Christ.

## CATACOMB OF SEBASTIAN

Address: Via Appia Antica 132. Opening hours 8:30-12:00 a.m. and 2:30-5:30 p.m. Closed on Sundays and in December. Tel. 06-7887035.

Transportation: bus 660 (leaves at the Largo dei Colli Albani which can be reached with Metro Linea A, station Colli Albani). Get off near the catacomb. There is a very small parking lot near the catacomb.

Tour includes: a visit to a series of subterranean galleries on the second level of the catacomb, comprising the so-called Piazzuola, an area with the remains of pagan mausolea including that of Clodius Hermes (see Chapter 2).

Description: The Sebastiano catacomb is one of the very few catacombs the location of which was never forgotten, not even during the Middle Ages and the Renaissance (see Chapter 1). The term "catacomb" was "born" here: originally it was a topographical indicator used to describe the area where later the Sebastiano catacomb was constructed. Only later did the term become generic and was used in the way it is still used today, to denote any large underground cemetery. The catacomb derives its name from Saint Sebastian, an early Christian saint who was tortured to death during the reign of the Emperor Dicoletian (A.D. 285-305) and who was buried in the catacomb.

In many ways, the evidence preserved in the Sebastiano catacomb is similar to that preserved in the other big early Christian catacombs of Rome. The Sebastiano catacomb consists of an enormous network of underground galleries that extends on four different levels. This network reflects the explosive growth of Rome's early Christian community in the fourth century. Originally, however, the Sebastiano catacomb was but a small complex, consisting of several independent pagan hypogea that were connected to another by means of underground galleries only gradually (for this development, see Chapter 2). Some of the underground hypogea were excavated using preexisting quarries.

A good example of what such pagan hypogea looked like has survived on the so-called Piazzuola. This is a small square that was originally located on the surface and that contains the facades of three pagan hypogea, among them that of Clodius Hermes (the one on the left, see also Chapter 2). The hypogeum of Clodius Hermes was Christianized at a later stage through the addition, on its facade, of scenes taken from the New Testament (scholarly opinion is divided over the identification of these scenes). The hypogeum next to it (the middle hypogeum) belonged to the family of the *Innocentiores*. It is interesting because it contains a graffito with the term *ichtus* ("fish," on the meaning of this term, see Chapter 3). The pagan family graves on the Piazzuola provide us with good evidence for a phenomenon described earlier (see Chapter 2), namely, the third century custom to extend a mausoleum that was located above ground by means of an underground extension.

Around the middle of the third century, the Piazzuola was covered in order to create space for a series of constructions that were located some 7 meters higher than the Piazzuola and whose main purpose was to commemorate the apostles Peter and Paul (fig. 42). Even though Peter had originally been buried on the Vatican hill, and Paul on the Via Ostiense, literary sources seem to suggest that their mortal remains (or parts thereof) were temporarily transferred in the third century to the area on top of the Piazzuola. The relics of Peter and Paul were probably stored in one of the buildings that was constructed here. In another building located at the site and dating to the same general period, the so-called *Triclia*, funerary meals seem to have been taking place. That such meals must have enjoyed popularity and that large amounts of people flocked to the site follows from the fact that the walls of the *Triclia* have been covered by graffiti and in which pilgrims made sure to invoke both Peter and Paul (the graffiti can still be seen behind a protective layer of glass).

In the early fourth century, a new round of construction followed at this site. A basilica was constructed on top of the *Triclia* and the building containing the bones of Peter and Paul. Not surprisingly, this basilica was given the name *basilica apostolorum* (literally "basilica of the apostles;" later it was also called basilica of San Sebastiano). The basilica's function was funerary. This is evident from the many graves that were installed in the basilica's floor as well as from the

Fig. 42. Sebastiano catacomb. Graffiti left by pilgrims on the site where the earthly remains of the apostles Peter and Paul were temporarily buried.

mausolea that were constructed directly against it on its outer walls (note that the present basilica is smaller than the original one and dates to the seventeenth century).

Only after the martyr Sebastian had been buried in one of the crypts of the catacomb did the Sebastiano catacomb develop into an underground early Christian cemetery of respectable proportions. It was during this time that architects also improved access to Sebastian's crypt by means of separate staircases (one for pilgrims entering the crypt and one for those leaving it) as well as a lucernarium that connected the crypt to the basilica above it (this lucernarium has been sealed again).

In the Sebastiano catacomb fewer wall paintings have been preserved than in other early Christian catacombs such as the Domitilla and Callisto catacombs. Of the few paintings that have survived in this catacomb, a rendering of the story of Jonah deserves special attention. Next to the entrance to the catacomb there also exists a small museum with inscriptions and sarcophagi that were discovered in the catacomb. The famous sarcophagus illustrating the life of Lot can unfortunately not be seen during regular visits.

## CATACOMB OF DOMITILLA

Address: Via delle Sette Chiese 282. Opening hours: 8:30-12:00 a.m. and 2:30-5:00 p.m.; closed on Tuesdays. Tel. 06-5110342. Fax 06-5135461.

Transportation: bus 218 (leaves at the Piazza S. Giovanni in Laterano, near Metro Linea A, station San Giovanni). Get off at the Fosse Ardeatine and then on foot to the entrance of the catacomb at the Via delle Sette Chiese.

Tour includes: the basilica of Nereus and Achilleus (fourth century A.D.); the hypogeum of the Flavii (late second century A.D.) and subterranean galleries with wall paintings dating to the third and fourth centuries.

Description: The Domitilla catacomb was first discovered in the sixteenth century by Bosio, who almost died there (see Chapter 1). G.B. de Rossi rediscovered the catacomb in the nineteenth century and spent many years there trying to elucidate the history of this enormous underground cemetery. With its galleries totaling more than 15 kilometers and containing many wonderfully preserved examples of early Christian wall painting, the Domitilla catacomb is one of the most fascinating early catacombs in the vicinity of Rome.

The catacomb derives its present name from an inscription that documents that in antiquity the area where the catacomb developed belonged to the *Domitilla* family. It is conceivable – although in no way certain – that in due course some members of this Domitilla family converted to Christianity and these people then put their lands at the disposal of Rome's early Christian community so that these grounds could be used for funerary purposes. It should be stressed that this explanation is just a hypothesis. Ancient sources indicate that originally the catacomb was not at all known as Domitilla catacomb, but rather as catacomb of Nereus and Achilleus (two saints that are buried here) or, alternatively, as the catacomb of Petronilla (another saint buried in the catacomb).

The Domitilla catacomb is located in an area that is rich in funerary monuments. In its earliest phase, the catacomb consisted of seven separate hypogea that all had separate entrances and that are referred to today using the names of the Roman families that were originally buried in them.

These hypogea came into existence in the course of the second and early third centuries. They are all of pagan origin.

The most famous of these hypogea is known as the "hypogeum of the Flavii" (fig. 43). This name derives from a fragmentary inscription that was discovered in the hypogeum by de Rossi. De Rossi reconstructed the inscription as referring to the family of the *Flavii*, that is a wealthy Roman

Fig. 43. Domitilla catacomb. Water well near the region of the Flavii.

family known from literary sources. Such sources indicate that some members of this family may have converted to Christianity early on, that is already in the late first century A.D. The "hypogeum of the Flavii" consists of a long, broad gallery with large niches on both sides. In these niches, sarcophagi were installed. The entrance to the hypogeum, which was originally located above ground, was made of brick. To the left of this entry a small room can be found that contains a well and benches. This room was probably used for funerary banquets. Such banquets were organized to commemorate the dead (they were called *refrigeria*). On the walls of the hypogeum itself one encounters wall paintings that are characteristic of the third century. They belong to a pictorial style known as the red-green linear style. Paintings of this type consists of red and green lines that subdivide a white surface into smaller fields that contain various kinds of decorative motifs such as animals or people. It is particularly interesting to note that these paintings were christianized in the course of time through the addition of Old Testament scenes including Daniel in the lions' den and a representation of Noah (visible at the farthest end of the "hypogeum of the Flavii").

To the right of the entrance to the "hypogeum of the Flavii" can be found the "Cubiculum of Amor and Psyche." It contains third-century wall paintings that help to document the popularity of bucolic and idyllic themes in early Christian art (see Chapter 3).

It was not until the fourth century that the Domitilla catacomb was used in a systematic fashion for the burial of large groups of people. It was only at that time that underground galleries began to get constructed on a large scale, as a result of which the catacomb developed into an enormous underground cemetery consisting of four different levels. Of all these underground levels, level two is the oldest.

The Domitilla catacomb is especially famous for its wall paintings. These wall paintings date in part to the third century (the Old Testament phase) and in part to the fourth (New Testament phase). Particularly interesting are a painting with the *fossor* Diogenes on it, as well as a representation of Jesus surrounded by saints and apostles (an example of the christological tendency discussed previously, see Chapter 3).

The basilica dedicated to the Saints Nereus and Achilleus dates, in its present shape, to the late fourth century. It has been decorated with archaeological materials from the catacomb. It also contains the fragments of an inscription erected by Damasus and meant to commemorate these saints. Nereus and Achilleus were martyrs who died during the persecutions under Diocletian (A.D. 284-305). The tomb in which they were buried was located at the spot where the apse of the present-day basilica is located (the original tomb was consciously removed to make room for the apse of the basilica). It is near this basilica that the cubiculum of Veneranda and Petronilla can be found. This cubiculum contains a very important early Christian wall painting that shows how Veneranda is led into Paradise by Petronilla (tradition has it that Petronilla was the daughter of Peter; the painted inscription refers to her as a martyr). Veneranda's cubiculum is part of a privileged zone *retro sanctos* that contains the cubicula of the rich and famous and that was located around the grave/basilica of the saints Nereus and Achilleus.

## CATACOMB OF PRISCILLA

Address: Via Salaria 430. Opening hours: 8:30-12:00 p.m. and 2:30-5:00 p.m. Closed on Mondays and in February. Fax. 06-86206272.

Transportation: bus 56 (leaves at Piazza Venezia), 57 (leaves at Stazione Termini) and 319 (stazione Termini). Get off at Piazza Priscilla.

Tour includes: a tour through the galleries belonging to the catacomb's upper level and a visit to the Capella Greca.

Description: The Priscilla catacomb is one of the oldest early Christian cemeteries in Rome. As is evident from the itineraries (see Chapter 1), already in the early Middle Ages people frequently visited this catacomb because it contained a great number of graves belonging to famous early Christian martyrs and popes.

The Priscilla catacomb consists of an extensive network of underground galleries on two levels. The building history of the Priscilla catacomb is similar to that of many other early Christian catacombs of Rome. Thus, the catacomb is located in an area that had been used for burial long before the catacomb was first constructed. Although we know fairly little about the tombs that once existed on the surface in this area, it is nevertheless clear that in the course of the second century these tombs were enlarged through underground additions. Such additions were made using preexisting cavities and quarries. Evidence for the one-time existence of such quarries can still be seen near the catacomb's entrance. Thus far, archaeologists have identified the remains of at least five hypogea in this area. One of these was used to bury the deceased members of a senatorial family named the *Acilii*.

An inscription found in their hypogeum indicates that Priscilla (the woman after whom the catacomb was later named) was a member of this family. A catacomb began to develop at the site when mentioned hypogea were enlarged by means of underground galleries that connected the hypogea to one another. That the builders of these galleries made use of a preexisting network of cisterns and water channels follows from the tubular shape of some of these galleries (on this issue, see also Chapter 2).

In the Priscilla catacomb important early Christian material remains have been preserved. Among these is the so-called *Capella Greca* or Greek chapel which belongs to the catacomb's earliest phase (it derives its name from two Greek inscriptions that were discovered here). The Capella Greca forms part of a larger area referred to by scholars as the *cryptoporticus* (literally, the hidden or underground portico). This area is especially interesting because of its wall paintings (fig. 44). On the cryptoporticus' back wall, on top of the central apse, a famous representation of the *fractio panis* (the breaking of the bread) can be seen. In this painting seven people have been rendered. They are seated around a table on which a chalice and a plate with fish has been placed. To the left and to the right of the table, baskets with bread were added. Although we do not know exactly what kind of meal the painter had in mind (a funerary meal, a Eucharistitic meal, or a heavenly meal?) it would seem that this representation contains a conscious allusion to the New Testament (the feeding of the five thousand, see Matthew 14:13-21 and parallels). Keeping in mind the nature of the wall painting and taking into account, moreover, that benches were constructed along the walls of the cryptoporticus, archaeologists have argued that the funerary rite most frequently performed in the Capella Greca was that of the *refrigerium*.

Other wall paintings that have been preserved in the Capella Greca finally also deserve our attention. They are good examples of the Old Testament phase of early Christian art. Among the scenes represented can be found: Moses drawing water from the rock, Susanna and the elders, the three

Fig. 44. Priscilla catacomb. Capella Greca with several scenes taken from the Old Testament.

Hebrews in the fiery furnace, the sacrifice of Isaac, Daniel in the lions' Den, and Noah and his Ark. The New Testament scenes that occur here include: the healing of the lame, the raising of Lazarus from the dead, and the Adoration of the Magi.

Interesting wall paintings can also be found in other parts of the Priscilla catacomb. They include a representation of a woman with child and a prophet, possibly a representation of a Madonna with child, and the prophet Balaam. In the same general area one also encounters a wall painting with a rendition of the Annunciation. Although it is hard to date these paintings with precision, the presence of a representation of "the Good Shepherd," of Jonah, and of bucolic and idyllic motifs seems to indicate that a third century dating for all these paintings is a reasonable assumption.

Not far from these paintings, we finally encounter the late third century "Cubiculum of the *Velatio*." It contains an arcosolium with a painted representation of a veiled woman with arms raised (a typical way of illustrating the act of prayer). To the left of this painting another depiction of the same woman can be found, this time during a wedding ceremony which also involves a bishop (he performs the wedding; the Latin *velare* means "to veil"). To the right we find yet another representation of the same woman. This time she is seated and carries a child (in the past, this painting was interpreted as Madonna with child). The "cubiculum of the *velatio*" is particularly rich in terms of the wall paintings that have survived there: it also contains a series of wall paintings that belong to the Old Testament phase in early Christian art. These wall paintings include a rendering of the three Hebrews in the fiery furnace, of the sacrifice of Isaac and of the story of Jonah. On the ceiling can be found a representation of a ram bearer or "Good Shepherd."

In the fourth century, the Priscilla catacomb began to be used for burials on a massive scale. From this time onwards, the catacomb developed into a large communal cemetery with long underground galleries containing numerous graves. Many of these galleries were excavated in a regular fashion, following the "fishbone" system (see Chapter 2).

## CATACOMB OF AGNESE

Address: Via Nomentana 349. Opening hours: 9:00-12:00 a.m. and 4:00-6:00 p.m. Closed on Sundays and on Monday Afternoon. Tel. 06-86205456. Fax. 06-8610840.

Transportation: busses 36 (stazione Termini), 60 (leaves at piazza Venezia), 137 (Via XX Settembre). Get off on the Via Nomentana, near San Agnese.

Tour includes: a visit to a series of subterranean galleries.

Description: The Agnese catacomb is located below a fourth century church and can be entered through this church. The entrance to the church (a long staircase) is decorated with inscriptions that derive from the catacomb.

The catacomb and church owe their name to a certain Agnes, a Roman girl who died during the persecutions of the third century. Pope Damasus composed an inscription in her honor. The inscription is exhibited along mentioned staircase.

Like so many of the other Roman catacombs, the Agnese catacomb is located in an area that had long been used for burial and in which many tombs and mausolea could be found on the surface. As a result of recent excavations we now know that this area contained pagan tombs that were used for both cremations and inhumations. Some of the pagan building materials were later reused in the catacomb. That this is so is particularly evident in region IV of the Agnese catacomb.

The Agnese catacomb can be subdivided into four subterranean regions of which region I is the oldest (fig. 45). In all these regions wall paintings do not occur very frequently. The inscriptions that have been recovered in various parts of

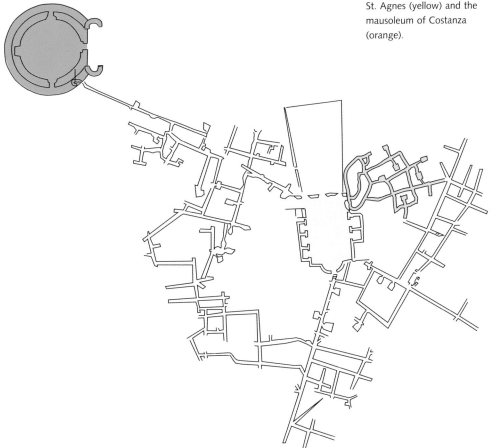

Fig. 45. Plan of the Agnese catacomb, showing the Area I (in blue), the basilica of St. Agnes (yellow) and the mausoleum of Costanza (orange).

the catacomb are the most important source of information concerning the Agnese catacomb.

The holy Agnes was probably buried in a section of the catacomb that was destroyed upon the construction of a fourth century basilica that was dedicated to her memory. Some traces of the area where Agnes was originally deposited have survived, however. They can be recognized because of the high concentration of simple graves – a good example of the custom of having one's mortal remains interred near the grave of a famous martyr (on this custom, see also Chapter 2).

A visit to the site of the Agnese catacomb is not complete without a visit to the nearby mausoleum of Santa Costanza. This fourth century building was designed as imperial mausoleum. It contains a series of interesting and important mosaics.

## VATICAN NECROPOLIS

Address: Ufficio Scavi della Reverenda Fabbrica di S. Pietro. This office is located to the left of St. Peter's. It can be reached by entering this part of the Vatican (go under the arch, past the Swiss guard) and then by keeping to the right. In order to visit this necropolis, one needs to apply in writing for a permit. This can be done on the spot, using a preprinted form. Normally, a visit to this necropolis is possible only on the day following the application.

Transportation: bus 64 (leaves at stazione Termini) or Metro Linea A, station Ottaviano and then to the Vatican on foot.

Tour includes: a visit to the pagan necropolis under basilica of St. Peter's and a visit to the grave of Peter.

Description: Below St. Peter's there exist several hollow spaces that can be visited by tourists and pilgrims (fig. 46). On the first subterranean level, directly below the basilica, one encounters the so-called *sacre grotte vaticane*. These "grottoes" can be entered from St. Peter's. They consist of a series of chapels that contain the graves of many popes. Under these *grotte*, on a still deeper level, the remains of an important pagan necropolis, known as the Vatican necropolis, have come to light. A visit to this necropolis is possible, but one needs to acquire a special permit (for details, see above). Although the necropolis is partially visible from the *grotte*, it cannot be entered via these. A separate entrance is located to the left of St. Peter's.

Fig. 46. Cross section of St. Peter's basilica. Below the basilica (upper level) can be found the *sacre grotte vaticane*. On the lower level remains of a pagan and early Christian necropolis containing the grave of St. Peter have been found.

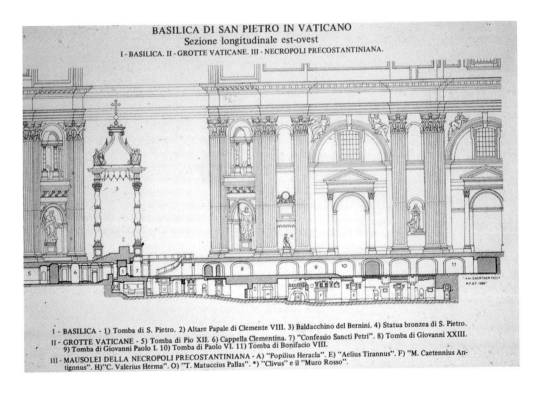

BASILICA DI SAN PIETRO IN VATICANO
Sezione longitudinale est-ovest
I - BASILICA. II - GROTTE VATICANE. III - NECROPOLI PRECOSTANTINIANA.

I - BASILICA - 1) Tomba di S. Pietro. 2) Altare Papale di Clemente VIII. 3) Baldacchino del Bernini. 4) Statua bronzea di S. Pietro.
II - GROTTE VATICANE - 5) Tomba di Pio XII. 6) Cappella Clementina. 7) "Confessio Sancti Petri". 8) Tomba di Giovanni XXIII. 9) Tomba di Giovanni Paolo I. 10) Tomba di Paolo VI. 11) Tomba di Bonifacio VIII.
III - MAUSOLEI DELLA NECROPOLI PRECOSTANTINIANA - A) "Popilius Heracla". E) "Aelius Tirannus". F) "M. Caetennius Antigonus". H)"C. Valerius Herma". O) "T. Matuccius Pallas". *) "Clivus" e il "Muro Rosso".

The Vatican necropolis dates to the first and second centuries A.D. It contains interesting evidence that helps us to better understand the process that led from the custom of cremating the dead to that of inhuming them. In addition, the evidence preserved here is important to help document that the christianization of the Roman Empire and its pagan population did not occur overnight, but rather was the result of a gradual process.

Originally, the tombs that make up the Vatican necropolis were located in the open air. These tombs were located on both sides of an alley (this is the same alley as the one used during visits to the Vatican necropolis). In the mausolea that can be found on the south side of mentioned alley, one finds evidence for the shift to inhumation from cremation: while in the urns that were set into walls ashes were stored, the arcosolia were reserved for inhumation, that is, for the interment of complete bodies. In the mausolea on the north side of the alley, on the other hand, urns have disappeared almost entirely. The absence of such urns means that these northern mausolea date to a slightly later period, namely the time that inhumation had completely replaced cremation as the most popular form of burial.

Inscriptions suggest that it was in the beginning of the third century that Christians began to use this necropolis. The Christianization of existing mausolea is evident, for example, in mausoleum M. This was a pagan mausoleum that belonged to the family of the *Julii*. It was christianized in the third century through the addition of an iconography which is typically Christian and characteristic of the earliest phase of Christian art. Among the topics represented here one encounters the story of Jonah, a ram bearer ("Good Shepherd"), and a fisher surrounded by vine leafs (bucolic and idyllic motifs). On the ceiling of this mausoleum a famous mosaic has been preserved. It contains a representation of a figure with a nimbus. Some scholars see in this person a representation of the pagan sun god Helios. But others reject such an identification, arguing instead that this is one of the oldest representations of a Christ with nimbus (note that the nimbus was not invented by Christian artists, but was already in use in pagan iconographic contexts).

The tomb that possibly contained the bones of Peter can be found at the western end of the Vatican necropolis. The history and archaeology of the area where Peter's grave has been found is fairly complex. The grave itself is innocuous. It was a simple tomb that was excavated into the ground. It was located in an area that contained some thirty other graves of this simple type (the so-called *formae*). In the course of the second century, this area was enclosed by mausolea, that is, by graves of a much more monumental nature.

Upon the construction of these mausolea, a supporting wall was also built. Because of its color, this supporting wall is known in the scholarly literature as the red wall. This wall contained, near the site where Peter's grave was located, three niches of which two were located above ground, and the third one under the surface. Near these niches archaeologists found a Greek graffito. It dates to the second or early third century A.D. and has been deciphered as reading ΠΕΤΡ (= Petr. = Peter). The niches above ground were decorated with columns and a lintel. They are normally identified as the "tropaeum of Gaius." This appellation derives from the Church Father's Eusebius' *Ecclesiastical History* (2.25.5-7). In this *Ecclesiastical History* Eusebius observes that he had heard from a certain Gaius that in the second century there existed, on top of the graves of the apostles Peter and Paul, *tropaia* (literally "memorials" – hence the somewhat misleading name "the tropaium of Gaius").

In the grave under the niches that decorate the "tropaium of Gaius," archaeologists have discovered bones. Some scholars believe these bones to be the mortal remains of Peter, but others question such an identification. One of the arguments used against this identification is that among the many graffiti left by pilgrims on walls in this area, the name Peter is completely absent (in these graffiti, Christograms, on the other hand, appear very frequently).

Upon the construction of the basilica of St. Peter's under Constantine (that is the basilica that preceded the present basilica), the Vatican necropolis was partially destroyed and partially covered. During these building activities, the apse of the new basilica was constructed directly above Peter's grave as marked by the "tropaium of Gaius." More precisely, the upper niche of the tropaium was removed as a result of which the presbytery of the church was now located some 40 cm. above the second niche (this niche was no longer visible). In the basilica itself, a canopy marked the spot where, on a deeper level, the tropaium, i.e., the grave of Peter, was located. During building activities in the later Middle Ages, architects continued to respect the original site of the tropaium. When the present basilica of St. Peter's was constructed, Bernini's baldachin was arranged in such a way that it was located right on top of the site identified as the grave of St. Peter.

## MUSEO PIO CRISTIANO

Address: Part of the Vatican Museum. Entrance Viale Vaticano. Opening hours: from April 1 through October 31: 8:45 a.m.-4:45 p.m.; from November through March 31: 8:45 a.m.-1:45 p.m. Closed on Sundays and Holidays, with the exception of the last Sunday of the month when entrance is free. The Vatican museum is usually very crowded. The collection of the Pio Cristiano can be found on the right side, directly after entering the museum. The collection is not always open to the public. Tel. 06-69884947.

Transportation: bus 81 (leaves at piazza Venezia); 492 (stazione Termini). Get off at Piazzale Risorgimento.

Description: The Museo Pio Cristiano is the single most important museum in Rome insofar as early Christian antiquities are concerned. It contains a highly interesting collection of early Christian sarcophagi as well as an important collection of early Christian inscriptions. Here can be found one of the masterpieces of early Christian art, namely the sarcophagus of Junius Bassus (see Chapter 3). Other sarcophagi that can be found here include those with representations of the story of Jonah, the ram bearer, and sarcophagi of the typological type (see Chapter 3). A statue of "the Good Shepherd" can also be found in this museum. In addition, the Pio Cristiano contains a large collection of Jewish funerary inscriptions (see Appendix I). Most of these inscriptions derive from the Monteverde catacomb (now destroyed).

Early Christian antiquities including lamps and glass are also on display in the *Museo Sacro* of the *Biblioteca Apostolica Vaticana.* This museum is part of the Vatican museums.

CHAPTER 5

# Appendix

## I. The Jewish Catacombs

In Antiquity, Rome was home to one of the largest Jewish communities outside the Land of Israel. We do not know exactly when Jews first came to Rome to settle there. Evidence suggests that already in the first century B.C. Jews had taken up residence in the capital of the Roman Empire. In due course, the Roman-Jewish community grew. By the fourth century A.D. it was one of the largest and most prominent Jewish communities in this part of the Mediterranean.

The Roman-Jewish community has left behind many archaeological traces, most of them funerary in nature. Most of these archaeological finds derive from four Jewish catacombs and two Jewish hypogea that have been discovered near Rome, in the same general area where the early Christian catacombs can be found. Even though Antonio Bosio discovered the first Jewish catacomb in 1602, little was known about these Jewish catacombs until recently. The lack of interest in these Jewish archaeological materials was largely due to the apologetic approach that long characterized catacomb archaeology (see Chapter 1).

The Jewish catacombs of Rome are similar to the early Christian ones in that they too are located along the main Roman roads. One of these Jewish catacombs, the so-called Vigna Randanini catacomb is located directly South of the city, on the Via Appia Antica, between the Callisto and Sebastiano catacomb complexes. To the North of the ancient city, two further Jewish catacombs can be found under the Villa Torlonia along the Via Nomentana (fig. 47). On the city's

eastern side, along the Via Portuense, remains have been discovered of what appears to have been the largest of all Jewish catacombs of Rome, the Monteverde catacomb. This catacomb no longer exists, however. It was destroyed in the 1930s as a result of building activity at the site. Even though their exact location is presently unknown, two Jewish hypogea mentioned previously were also located along major arteries.

Also where it concerns their formal characteristics and their construction history, the Jewish and Christian catacombs of ancient Rome have much in common. Like the early Christian catacombs, the Jewish catacombs consist of long underground galleries and cubicula that contain loculi

Fig. 47. Villa Torlonia catacomb. Wall painting of the back wall of an arcosolium with seven branched candelabrum and open chest with scrolls.

and arcosolia graves.[1] Not infrequently, such galleries have been excavated using preexisting quarries (*arenaria*), cisterns and water channels.

The oldest Jewish catacombs are not catacombs in the proper sense of the word. Like the oldest early Christian catacombs, they consist of a series of separate hypogea that were eventually connected to one another. That this is so is especially evident in the case of the Vigna Randanini catacomb, with its irregular underground galleries. A look at the plan of this cemetery suggests that it was not constructed as a catacomb from the start. Initially, this area contained several underground hypogea that all had their own, separate entrances. As the need to create space for additional graves arose, galleries were excavated that were meant as extensions of these hypogea. In due course, such galleries were extended further and further, thus giving this underground cemetery the appearance of a catacomb. The Jewish Vigna Randanini catacomb thus helps to document the process we have described above (Chapter 2), namely the development that led, in the course of the second and third centuries, from the construction of small-size mausolea above ground to cemeteries of considerable size below ground.

Other Jewish catacombs, such as the two interconnected catacombs under the Villa Torlonia, on the other hand, date to a slightly later period in the history of catacomb architecture. The Jewish Villa Torlonia catacombs are real catacombs in the sense that they have been specifically designed as such

---

[1] The only exception is formed by some graves in the Vigna Randanini catacomb. The graves in question are so-called *kokhim*. These graves stand out because they are not cut parallel to the wall as loculi, but rather at right angles. They belong to a type that was widespread in the eastern Mediterranean. but that further West occurs only in the Jewish catacombs of Rome.

from the start. As is evident from the systematic way in which the galleries have been laid out and the manner in which the graves have been arranged, the Villa Torlonia catacombs are comparable to several of the larger early Christian catacombs of Rome dating to the same period, namely the fourth century. All these catacombs – Jewish and Christian – were designed from the very start as large communal underground cemeteries.

The formal similarity between the Jewish and the early Christian catacombs of Rome helps to explain why the Jewish catacombs of Rome do not predate the Christian ones, as some scholars have maintained. The archaeological materials from the Jewish catacombs date to roughly the same period as those deriving from the Christian catacombs, that is, the period from the late second through the fifth centuries A.D.

Just as was the case with the early Christian community, we do not know where the Jewish community of Rome buried its dead before they began using hypogea and catacombs for this purpose. At present we do not have the archaeological means to identify these early Jewish burials. The reason for this is simple: symbols and inscriptions that could help us identify remains as Jewish do not seem to have been in use among Roman Jews during the period predating the third century A.D.

The inscriptions from the Jewish catacombs of Rome are an extremely important source of information. To date, some 600 Jewish funerary inscriptions have been recovered. These inscriptions help to throw light on a whole range of issues. First and foremost, they permit us to identify the catacombs in which they have been found as Jewish. These inscriptions also allow us to conclude that in the Jewish catacombs of Rome only Jews and proselytes (converts to Judaism) were laid to rest. Such evidence suggests that when it came to burial, Jews preferred to be interred in their own cemeteries, among their co-religionists. Jewish funerary inscriptions indicate that the Jewish community was very important in the daily lives of those buried here. In many Jewish gravestones we thus find references to the role someone fulfilled within the Jewish community when still alive, such as "head of the community" or "scribe." Also frequently included are adjectives that describe someone's personality or character. Again, adjectives of a Jewish or religious nature are most popular, including "pious" and "lover of the law."

Although it may be clear, therefore, that the inscriptions stress the Jewishness of those commemorated in them, they nevertheless also provide us with a glimpse of how Jews interacted with non-Jews in daily life. Most remarkably, the majority of these inscriptions have been composed in Greek and Latin, that is, the languages most commonly spoken in Rome at the time, rather than in Hebrew or Aramaic. The languages of these inscriptions, along with their linguistic features, indicate that the Jews who ordered them constituted a group that from a linguistic point of view was completely integrated into late antique society at large. That this is so becomes further evident when we look at the names appearing in the Jewish inscriptions. Although names of biblical origin occur in some of them, many Jewish inscriptions carry names that are thoroughly Roman in terms of their formal appearance. The names in question are of Latin or Greek derivation and consist of three parts, namely a first name, a family name, and nickname (the so-called *tria nomina*, a typically Roman name-giving system).

Other archaeological materials that inform us about the Jewish community of ancient Rome include wall paintings and sarcophagi. Only a few wall paintings have been preserved in the Jewish catacombs of Rome. In them, we encounter the same emphasis on "things Jewish" as in the inscriptions. Thus representations of symbols that are typically Jewish predominate. Such symbols include the menorah (seven-branched candlestick, a reference to the Temple in Jerusalem), the Aron (a chest containing scrolls), and the lulav (palm branch) and ethrog (citrus, both symbols are references to the Jewish festival of Tabernacles). It is remarkable that narrative scenes or cycles taken from the Hebrew Bible do not appear on either the wall paintings or on the sarcophagi from the Jewish catacombs of Rome – this in contrast to the early Christian catacombs in which scenes taken from the Old and, later, the New Testament were very popular (see Chapter 3). Such divergences between Jewish and early Christian art are interesting because they suggest that these communities had different kinds of iconographic preferences.

In the Jewish catacombs of Rome only a few sarcophagi have survived. Despite the fragmentary state in which these sarcophagi have been preserved, they nevertheless permit us to conclude that Jews were similar to Christians in that they also ordered these stone containers from Roman workshops that catered to a variety of customers (see Chapter 3). A good example of this can be found in the Museo Nazionale Romano (Thermae Museum). There a Jewish sarcophagus fragment is exhibited that dates to the early fourth century (fig. 48). It belongs to a type of sarcophagus known as Season sarcophagus. Season sarcophagi such as this one were decorated with personifications of the seasons (hence the name). Being extremely popular, these sarcophagi were mass-produced. The only part that was not mass-produced was the central *clipeus* or tondo in which a portrait of the deceased or a deceased couple would be sculpted. In case of the Jewish piece, however, such portraits were dispensed with. Instead, a menorah – in Antiquity Judaism's most prominent symbol –

Fig. 48. Detail of a Jewish sarcophagus from Rome, containing the representation of a menorah.

was placed here, thus transforming this typically Roman sarcophagus into a product that Jews too could find acceptable and desirable.

It is this process of transformation that is characteristic of how Jews in third- and fourth-century Rome coped with the realities of daily life: on the one hand they made use of what was commonly available, yet, on the other hand, they did not adapt local fashions slavishly; instead, they adapted what was available in such a way as to express their identity as Jews. Thus they bought sarcophagi that were manufactured in Roman workshops, but only after Jewish symbols had been placed on them. Along similar lines, they made use of painting techniques that were typically Roman, but only to paint walls with symbols that were specifically and exclusively Jewish. They spoke the language everyone else in Rome spoke, but they did so to express ideas and beliefs that are unmistakably Jewish. Even the Jewish catacombs should be viewed in this manner: they were underground cemeteries that came into existence in exactly the same period as the early Christian catacombs of Rome, yet even though they came into existence as a result of the same historical forces and under the same technical conditions, the Jewish catacombs of Rome were designed specifically as cemeteries in which Jews – and Jews only – were to be laid to rest.

## II. Early Christian Inscriptions

In the early Christian catacombs of Rome some 40,000 funerary inscriptions have been preserved (fig. 49). Like the Jewish funerary inscriptions, these early Christian inscriptions inform us about a whole range of issues for which information is not readily available from other sources. The majority of these early Christian inscriptions are written in Latin. Most of them were erected in the fourth century A.D or later.

Fig. 49. Selection of early Christian funerary inscriptions with Christian symbols such as the dove, the anchor, and the Chi-Rho monogram.

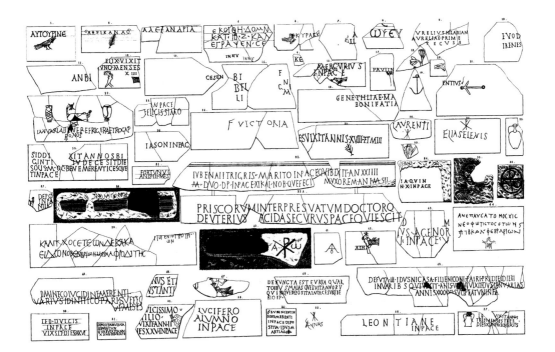

Although the information contained in individual inscriptions is at times very limited, these inscriptions still permit us to know a lot about the world of early Christianity. Because they have survived in large numbers, it becomes possible to look for patterns that can be traced by studying this evidence comprehensively rather than on the level of the individual inscriptions.

As a result of the many studies that have been carried out in this particular area, we now know that only a few early Christian inscriptions predate the fourth century A.D. Such "early" inscriptions are usually very short (they often contain the name of the deceased only), and they are mostly written in Greek rather than in Latin (this usage is explained by referring to the fact that well into the fourth century the liturgy in Rome's early Christian churches was held in Greek). Another characteristic of these early inscriptions that marks the beginning of early Christian epigraphy is that formulae of pagan derivation occur in them. Most interesting in this respect is the abbreviation *DM*. This abbreviation, which stands for *Dis Manibus* or "To the Gods of the Underworld" was used frequently in pagan inscriptions dating to the first and second centuries A.D. It hardly needs stressing that this phrase is not appropriate in a Christian context. That it occurs all the same, at least during this early period, must be seen as yet another piece of evidence for a phenomenon we have described earlier (see Chapter 2), namely, the fact that the Christianization of Rome's pagan population was a gradual process: as people began to convert to Christianity, they not only had to learn about a new religion, they also had to learn how to give up their pagan heritage.

With the large-scale Christianization of the Roman Empire starting in the fourth century also begins a new period in early Christian inscriptional practices in Rome.

From now on inscriptions are no longer carved in Greek. Latin becomes the predominant language. From a linguistic point of view, such inscriptions are interesting because they allow us to reconstruct, from a rather unusual angle, the history of the Latin language during this period. Scholars refer to the Latin that appears in these inscriptions with the term late Latin or, more frequently still, with the term vulgar Latin. The Latin in these inscriptions clearly differs from the Latin one encounters in inscriptions dating to an earlier period, in terms of vocabulary, phraseology, and syntax. The frequent use of abbreviations is yet another characteristic of these early Christian inscriptions in Latin.

The early Christian inscriptions in Latin are interesting also in other respects. With regard to name giving, continuity with the past is perhaps the most outstanding characteristic. Such continuity can best be explained by pointing out, once again, that most converts to Christianity were people of pagan origin who carried over practices and behaviors to which they had been long accustomed. Thus the typically Roman *tria nomina*-system (see above) occurs frequently in early Christian inscriptions. Early Christian inscriptions also help to document how in late antiquity this system started to disintegrate: first the *tria nomina* were replaced by *duo nomina* (double names), and then they made room for a system consisting of single names only. Such a single-name system became so popular in late antiquity that it could be found in 80% of all early Christian inscriptions from Rome that were carved in Latin. Biblical names, on the other hand, appear in these early Christian inscriptions only in exceptional cases. Names derived from the New Testament, including Paul, Peter, John and, to a lesser extent, Andrew and Maria, can be found more often in early Christian inscriptions, but again, they do not occur very frequently.

In contrast to the Jewish funerary inscriptions in which emphasis is placed on the role played by the deceased in the (Jewish) community, early Christian inscriptions generally lack references of this kind. What is included are references to occupations. Such references allow us to learn more about the socio-economic status of the people buried in the early Christian catacombs of Rome. References to beliefs or dogmas that are typically Christian have also been included in these inscriptions, but such references are usually short. Typically Christian is the view of death not as the end of this life but as the beginning of the next one. Names such as *Anastasia/Anastasius* and *Redempta/Redemptus* indicate that Christian beliefs concerning the afterlife were sometimes expressed onomastically, that is, in names. Due to the concise manner in which they have been formulated, it is fairly difficult to draw up a coherent picture of how the people commemorated in these inscriptions viewed the afterlife. Still, even a cursory look at these inscriptions helps to make clear that in this respect early Christian inscriptions differ notably from pagan ones: in the latter, emphasis is almost always placed exclusively on someone's exploits in this world and little or nothing is said about someone's fate in the hereafter.

Scholars have tried to use the evidence provided by the inscriptions for a variety of other purposes, for example, to reconstruct aspects of the demography of Rome's early Christian population. Many inscriptions contain references to the age at death. Scholars have used such references to reconstruct the life expectancy patterns of those commemorated in these inscriptions. A comparison of the evidence from the inscriptions with evidence that is statistically and demographically reliable such as the Life Expectancy Tables published by the United Nations, however, indicates that the inscriptions cannot serve as a reliable guide with regard to demography.

Subsequent research has shown that cultural factors determine the pattern of commemoration in these inscriptions. Thus, in inscriptions carved in Greek references to age at death are included when the deceased had reached old age. Latin inscriptions on the other hand tend to include a reference to age at death only when the person commemorated in it died young.

The early Christian inscriptions erected by Pope Damascus (A.D. 366-384) fall into a separate category (see also Chapter 2). Painted and incised inscriptions, the so-called dipinti and graffiti form another subcategory. Painted inscriptions are a fairly common occurrence on graves in the catacombs (fig. 50). Such inscriptions provided people who were not in

Fig. 50. Detail of a painted funerary inscription in Greek.

a position to order marble inscriptions with a cheap, yet very functional alternative. The incised inscriptions can be further subdivided into two groups. Some of these inscriptions were incised in the stucco that sealed off someone's grave at the time of burial, when the stucco was still wet. Other graffiti-inscriptions were scratched into stucco at a later point of time. Such inscriptions were often the work of pilgrims who visited the holy sites, such as the *Triclia* in the Sebastiano catacomb.

# GLOSSARY

**apse:** semicircular recess, often at the east end of a church

**apologists:** authors who defended the Christian faith by means of apologetic writings in which they tried to rebuff allegations made by their opponents

**arcosolium:** rectangular tomb cut into the rock, characterized by semicircular vault, see fig. 24

**arenarium:** sand quarry, often used for burial (secondary use)

**bucolic:** also idyllic: everything relating to life in the countryside

**catacomb:** subterranean cemetery, consisting of underground galleries and burial chambers

**clipeus:** literally "shield;" also tondo; motif frequently used on sarcophagi to frame the potraits of the deceased, see fig. 48

**christogram:** monogram consisting of the two Greek letters that form the first letters of the name of Christ, namely X (*chi*) and P (*rho*)

**crypt:** subterranean burial chamber

**cubiculum:** burial chamber (plural: cubicula)

**cremation:** the incineration of corpses (as opposed to inhumation)

**Dis Manibus:** pagan formula meaning "to the gods of the underworld", see fig. 29

**dipinto:** painted inscription (plural: dipinti), see fig. 50

**epigraphy:** study of inscriptions

**festoon:** chain of flowers and ribbons

**forma:** grave cut into the floor or living rock

**fossor:** person responsible for cutting the galleries and graves in the catacombs, see fig. 23

**graffito:** incised inscriptions (plural: graffiti), see fig. 42

**hypogeum:** subterranean family grave (plural: hypogea)

**ichthus:** Greek work for fish; an abbreviation of the phrase "Jesus Christ, Son of God, Savior", see fig. 29

**inhumation:** interment of corpse (as opposed to cremation)

**ketos:** seamonster, appears in early Christian art to illustrate the story of Jonah and the whale, see figs. 32, 33

**kriophoros:** rambearer, used in early Christian art to represent the Good Shepherd, see fig. 30, 31

**Late Antiquity:** the period from the third to sixth century A.D.

**liberti:** freed slaves

**loculus:** rectangular grave cut into the walls of the catacombs; the most common type of grave in the catacombs (plural: loculi), see fig. 24

**lucernarium:** light and air shaft (plural: lucernaria), see fig. 15

**mausoleum:** tomb located above ground (plural: mausolea)

**martyr:** blood witness

**mosaic:** type of decoration consisting of little stones or glass, see fig. 37

**necropolis:** city of the dead, graveyard

**nimbus:** halo

**ossuarium:** place or container used to store bones, see fig. 25

**pergola:** structure covered with climbing plants, often used in depictions of the story of Jonah, see figs. 32 and 33

**putti:** winged infants, also cupids, often depicted to illustrate the idyllic nature of the scene depicted, see fig. 28

**pozzolana:** vulcanic earth, used by the Romans to produce concrete

**refrigerium:** meal to commemorate the dead, see fig. 41

**retro sanctos:** area behind or near a martyr's grave

**sarcophagus:** stone container used for burial (plural: sarcophagi), see fig. 28

**tuff:** volcanic soil into which the catacombs were excavated, see fig. 14

**typology:** concept according to which events taking place in the Old Testament prefigure events in the New Testament, see fig. 38

**verus Israel:** the true Israel; a theological concept developed by Christian theologians to argue that Christianity was the one and only heir of the Covenant between God and the people of Israel

## SELECTED BIBLIOGRAPHY

### On the Catacombs

Ferrua, A., *The Unknown Catacomb. A Unique Discovery of Early Christian Art* (New Lanark: Geddes & Grosset, 1991)

Fink, J. and B. Asamer, *Die römischen Katakomben* (Mainz: Verlag Philipp von Zabern, 1997)

Fiocchi Nicolai, V. *et al.*, *Le catacombe cristiane di Rome. Origini, sviluppo, apparati decorativi, documentazione epigrafica* (Regensburg: Schnell & Steiner, 1998) (also forthcoming in an English translation)

Guyon, J., *Le cimitière aux deux lauriers. Recherches sur les catacombes romaines* (Rome: Pontificio Istituto di Archeologia Cristiana en École Française de Rome, 1987)

Nestori, A. *Repertorio topografico delle pitture delle catacombe romane* (Vatican City: Pontificio Istituto di Archeologia Cristiana, 1993)

Pergola, P. and P.M. Barbini, *Le catacombe romane. Storia e topografia* (Rome: Brettschneider, 1997)

Rutgers, L.V., *The Jews in Late Ancient Rome. Evidence of Cultural Interaction in the Roman Diaspora* (Leiden: Brill, 1995)

*id.*, *The Hidden Heritage of Diaspora Judaism. Essays on Jewish Cultural Identity in the Roman World* (Leuven: Peeters, 1998)

De Santis, L. and G. Biamonte, *Le catacombe di Roma* (Rome: Newton & Compton, 1997)

Testini, P., *Archeologia Cristiana. Nozioni generali dalle origini alla fine del sec. VI* (Bari: Edipuglia, 1981)

### On Early Christian Art

Belting, H., *Bild und Kult. Eine Geschichte des Bildes vor dem Zeitalter der Kunst* (München: Beck, 1990)

Deichmann, W.F., *Einführung in die christliche Archäologie* (Darmstadt: Wissenschaftliche Buchgesellschaft, 1983) (also available in an Italian translation)

Donati, A., *Dalla terra alle genti. La diffusione del cristianesimo nei primi secoli* (Milan: Electa, 1996) (catalogue of an exhibition)

Elsner, J., *Art and the Roman Viewer. The Transformation of Art from the Pagan World to Christianity* (Cambridge: Cambridge University Press, 1995)

Engemann, J., *Deutung und Bedeutung früchristlicher Bildwerke* (Darmstadt: Primus-Verlag, 1997)

Finney, P.C., *The Invisible God. The Earliest Christians on Art* (Oxford: Oxford University Press, 1994)

Koch, G., *Früchristliche Kunst. Eine Einführung* (Stuttgart: Verlag W. Kohlhammer, 1995)

Milburn, R., *Early Christian Art and Architecture* (Berkeley: University of California Press, 1988)

# INDEX

PRINTED ON PERMANENT PAPER • IMPRIME SUR PAPIER PERMANENT • GEDRUKT OP DUURZAAM PAPIER - ISO 9706

ORIENTALISTE, KLEIN DALENSTRAAT 42, B-3020 HERENT